LOST

in the

American Dream

LOST

in the *American Dream*

The costs, false promises and spiritual realities of living the American Dream

Dennis McDaniel

Tate Publishing & *Enterprises*

This title is also available as a Tate Out Loud product. Visit www.tatepublishing.com for more information.

Published by Tate Publishing & Enterprises, LLC
127 E. Trade Center Terrace | Mustang, Oklahoma 73064 USA
1.888.361.9473 | www.tatepublishing.com

Tate Publishing is committed to excellence in the publishing industry. The company reflects the philosophy established by the founders, based on Psalms 68:11,
"The Lord gave the word and great was the company of those who published it."

Cover design by Eddie Russell
Interior design by Lindsay B. Behrens

Published in the United States of America

ISBN: 978-1-60247-822-0
1. Christian Living 2. Practical Life 3. Contemporary Issues
07.09.26

Dedication

For Gary and Kathy Branch. Without their encouragement, this book would not have been written.

Table of Contents

Introduction

It was 1973. I was driving my battered Volkswagen down a street in Washington, D.C., moving through a furious rainstorm. Buckets of water poured down on the windshield, when suddenly one of the wipers flew off the car and into the street. I scrambled into the driving rain, retrieved the blade and inserted it back onto the car. One week later I paid cash to purchase a beautiful brand new 1973 Pontiac. I had been a poor boy from a poor town. No more. I was working in the nation's capital, had a law degree and my first job as an attorney. I had lots of ambition, money in the bank to purchase a new car, and I wanted my share of the American Dream.

But dreams seldom square with reality. They are often jumbled, disoriented and disconnected from real life. Life can't be lived in a dream. Reality explodes our fantasies. On the way home from the dealership, my beautiful new car began to squeak and creak, its beauty on the outside belied by poor assembly on the inside.

It is God who created us, looks after us, knows our hearts and provides for our care. God is love. The world is not love. The world is a "jealous provider," chary about what it gives, eager to take back what it has given. It imposes a price on whatever we want, never satisfied or content with what we achieve, always looking over its shoulder to bless someone who achieves more. The world's provision is never lasting, always in need of refill.

I have a card given to me by a local merchant, offering a free cup of coffee. That is the good news. The bad news is that I must purchase ten cups of coffee, at a cost of $18, to get my free cup of coffee. What the world gives with the right hand, it takes away with the left. Its provision always rests on the borderline of empty. Like the gasoline in a car, we must constantly repurchase more to keep things moving. But the need to make more money, to buy more things and to keep things moving can get very tiresome. Life becomes a treadmill we must run on to keep from falling behind and, if we slow down, we can collapse.

In my first job after law school, I worked in a litigation division with about fifteen lawyers. My colleagues were young, ambitious, anxious to climb the ladder of success, as I was. Over the years, I saw the toll ambition can have on a person's life. From that office, there were four disbarments; broken marriages; alcohol and substance abuse; a suicide; a criminal conviction; and, when I left D.C. twenty-six years later, a former colleague who was living in a homeless shelter.

After several years, I moved to another job, this time with a federal agency in Washington, D.C. There I drafted legislation, wrote signing statements for presidential signature, argued cases in federal courts and drafted congressional testimony for agency heads. I worked with people who were quoted in newspapers and seen on television. But career paths were stormy and the world provided no safe harbor for success. A botched assignment, a congressional election, a working relationship gone sour could turn a "star" into a "fallen star." It didn't matter how high one rose through the ranks, every person was susceptible to a fall. John Dean, legal counsel to President Nixon, wrote in his book, *Blind Ambition*, that the higher he climbed through the White House chain of command, the worse the moral climate got. When he got to the inner sanctum of the Oval Office, it was the foulest, most morally corrupt of all, he said.

Yet, success is a compelling part of the American Dream. At a high school class reunion, I was struck by how much conversation centered around how well one had succeeded since high school, as though the need to prove self-worth was a given: "I have an estate with a pool, and my son is climbing the corporate ladder," one said. Essentially: "I have succeeded; how about you?"

Christians are not exempt from this kind of peer pressure. How many times have you heard the expression, "He is living the American Dream" and wished it were you? The American Dream embodies a charmed life: a fancy car, an elegant house, 2.9 well-behaved children, dean's list, lots of money. Why should a Christian look away from this? But many do not see the spiritual costs that lie hidden in a quest to "have it all," and many do not pause to define, or to reflect, on that tantalizing word, "success."

We live in an age of rampant consumerism, with a "shop til you drop" mentality that has popularized "great deals" into quick solutions for a "better life." China and India have entered the "consumer-age" now, with billions of people wanting to buy more things for pleasure, satisfaction and leisure. At the same time, the planet's natural resource base is sending out signals that it is being stretched to the limit by soaring worldwide consumer demand for energy, water, food, and clean air, exacerbated by a world population growing by over 200,000 persons a day. God told us that we are to act as stewards of His creation, which He created in love. Habitat loss, global warming and wildlife extinction are providing evidence that man is not faithfully executing stewardship responsibilities and that, if our planet is not properly looked after and cared for, all living creatures could be adversely affected.

When I became a Christian, I expected to see significant differences in the way Christians perceived things and lived. But I saw that many, if not most, were caught up in the familiar American Dream themes: wanting the extravagant purchase; to earn the extra buck; to get ahead; to be successful; to get in on that "once in a lifetime investment opportunity." More than once, I heard a Christian refer to church as a good place for business contacts. And I saw the damage idolization of the "material" can inflict on the human heart. Madonna sang about the positives of being a "Material Girl," but the lyrics do not warn of the dangers a "material focus" can have on a marriage, family, financial well-being, mental and physical health.

The story is an ancient one. The Israelites worshipped a "golden calf" as god. But God pulverizes "golden calves" into a distasteful chalk the wayward must drink. He does the same today. The American Dream is not a manifestation of God's Truth, but a fanciful creation, materialistic in its origin, worldly in its presentation that can lead to great personal harm. We have heard about dysfunctional families, but what about dysfunctional Christians? What about churches that have lost their bearing because they took a wrong turn and followed the wrong shepherd? An unthinking pursuit of the American Dream can become a spiritual nightmare.

My Life with Cher

God created Adam and Eve as spiritual beings, in God's image. In Colossians 1:16, Jesus is identified as the Creator of all things. Thus, it is Jesus who formed Adam and Eve from the dust of the ground, who "breathed into Adam's nostrils" giving him life. The word "Spirit" translates from the Hebrew into the word "breath." Because God is Holy, Christ breathed His *Holy* Spirit into man. So man was created in the image of God, to be Holy (Gen. 2:7).

While man's inner being was inextricably connected to the presence of God's Spirit in him, man's flesh was shaped out of clay and molded into a personal appearance that, while beautiful, was by its nature dead, lifeless. Speak to a mound of clay, there will be no answer. Speak to a diamond ring on your finger, there will be no answer. The flesh counts for nothing (Jn 6:63) and can say nothing.

The world reverses this truth, putting importance on outer appearance, not on inner character. Consider how much newsprint is devoted to pictures of pretty faces, living in pretty homes, with pretty things, and people traveling to pretty places. Pretty persons, objects and places are pleasing to our eye, to our emotions. The world tells us that all we have to do to beautify our life is to beautify things around us: our furniture, skin, car, landscaping. But appearance can be manipulated.

One day I walked out of my office, thinking about a troublesome work assignment and paying little attention to where I was walking. When I looked up, I saw a man frantically waving his arms at me, and I saw the actress, Cher, with a very disgusted look on her face, mumbling to herself. I had wandered onto a movie set. Once shooting resumed, I learned why movie stars can look so attractive on the screen. The camera would roll for a few seconds, stop, and the makeup person would quickly walk up to Cher, comb her hair, apply makeup to her face, look closely at the result and, once satisfied, hastily retreat. The cameras would roll again for a few minutes, stop, and the assistant would hurriedly return, applying a comb to Cher here, a spray to Cher there, a dab to Cher where needed. Finished, she would walk away and filming would resume. That is the world. What we see is not always what we get. Beauty can be so temporal that, to keep it pretty, it needs makeup by the minute, if not by the second.

The world concentrates on the images of the seen, discounting the substance of the unseen, which includes God Himself. I didn't get to be in that movie, and the makeup artist paid no attention to me. Yet it was my appearance that day that was real, not dabbed, sprayed, fabricated and combed to look "split-second pretty." I was just another human being, standing on the street, sweltering in the reality of the Washington, D.C. heat and humidity, and that wouldn't have sold a ticket. Reality isn't pleasing to the world's eye. The world wants the camera to film beauty for beauty "sells." But reality has to be watched carefully, or it will displace beauty very quickly. To a camera's eye, a wrinkle can become a valley.

We have a spiritual camera on our hearts, which films for our consciences the personal flaws and imperfections of our inner beings, encoding to our brains the spiritual message of "falling short." God will change our heart if we ask Him to enter, but many do not extend the invitation. Rather, they choose to mask the heart, trusting that, if they can look pretty, they are pretty.

But man's spiritual problem is not "bad skin." The problem is a "bad heart." We are born with a "heart condition" the world can't cure with its face creams, tattoo artists, elegant houses, pleasure cruises, romantic songs, first class seating, body spas. Living the American Dream may put us in a pretty house, but it doesn't change a sinful heart. God dwells on the heart, washes away sin and His remedy is lasting, but one must ask Him to enter. Those who turn away from God do not receive God's cure, but they can count on receiving the devil's misery.

Fill Me Up Please

Let us turn now to the "Circle of Life."

God/Life

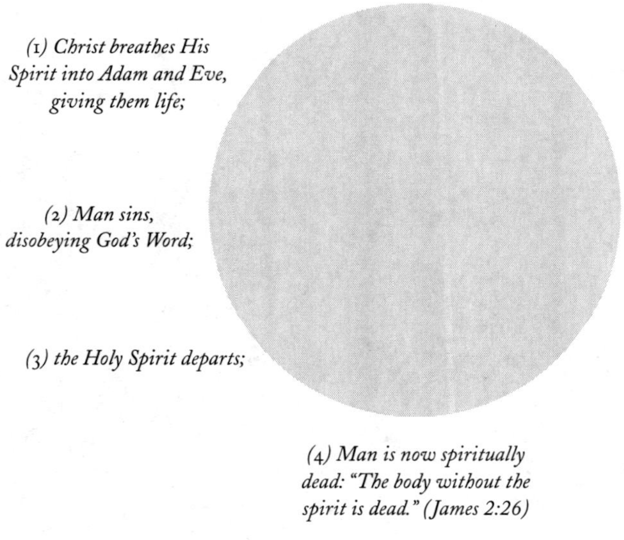

At the top of the circle is God, the creator of life, who holds life together, and who is "Holy, Holy, Holy" (Isa. 6:3). Going down the circle: (1) Christ gives man life, breathing His Spirit into him (Gen. 2:7). The word "Spirit" translates from the Hebrew into the word "breath." Give a person breath (Spirit) and he has life; take away breath (Spirit) and he dies. Hence, from the beginning, man's life was contingent on God's Spirit (breath) remaining in him. (2) Adam and Eve disobey God and fall into sin. (3) The Holy Spirit departs, for being a *Holy* Spirit, He will not dwell in sin. (4) Adam and Eve are now a shell of their former being—a "body without the spirit," and "the body without the spirit is *dead*" (James 2:26). Our heart testifies to this condition.

When I was growing up, and well into my adult life, I was puzzled by the stormy emotions of my behavior—the jealousy, anger, spite, meanness, selfishness that would erupt within me. I thought I must be different from others, that I had been born absent of some vital emotional linkage that would keep my temperament calm, my decision making flawless. I was incomplete inside and I knew it. I felt "dead" inside for it seemed that some vital connection to understanding and to living properly was missing. The Apostle Paul described this condition in Romans, saying that although he wanted to do right, something inside caused him to do wrong (Rom. 7:15–17). As a child, I didn't understand that "all have sinned and fall short of the glory of God" (Rom. 3:23). The Bible would have led me to that understanding. But the world pointed me away from that truth for years with its worldly fantasies of "fullness of life" without God.

The Lure of Beauty

Beautiful things are attractive to the eye, and those who can accumulate many beautiful things are "beautiful people," or so the world reasons. So, man naturally concludes that, if he is "empty" on the inside, "beauty" from the outside will fill up this "deadness" and make life good again. Satan showed Eve a beautiful thing, saying that by taking it into her life she would be more complete as a person. The world does the same today, portraying the things it wishes to sell us as life-giving, able to make us richer, stronger, happier, more beautiful. But the devil is in the details.

Many will recall the "Marlboro Man," who was seen on television commercials and billboards for many years. His image was a global marketing success: a strong, ruggedly handsome cowboy, on horseback in the wide-open spaces of the American West, smoking a Marlboro cigarette. The marketing link was a simple one: smoke a Marlboro, be a real man. But the image was far from the truth. Smoking can lead to cancer, and the "Marlboro Man" died of cancer, which he attributed to his many years of smoking cigarettes. An acquaintance of mine met the "Marlboro Man" shortly before he died and was shocked by what he saw, not the icon of strength and power portrayed on the billboards and on television, but a man whose body had withered away from disease and who had to struggle for every breath. No commercials portrayed this image.

The world sells its products beautifully packaged and presented with pretty models and perfect smiles. It has grasped a spiritual truth without even knowing it: that man hungers for "completion" as a person, that every person senses something "missing inside," a "big hole" in need of filling. Bring more riches into your life and the emptiness will go away, the American Dream tells us.

Things Will Fill the Hole

We are all familiar with holes. As children we learned that a hole can be filled by putting something into it. The world is very adept at telling us how to "fill our hole," to be "complete." "Buy this, buy that and your life will be changed for the better." Completeness is just a purchase away.

As I write this, I see an advertisement on the internet, a picture of an attractive couple holding hands, sitting on a yacht, and a caption reading: "Real people. Real success." They look so radiantly beautiful and happy that I am coaxed into their "picture dream" world. They have their "lives together" I say to myself. I conclude: "If that pretty couple with that fat bank account, sitting on that expensive yacht are 'real people' and have 'real success,' I want what they have." The advertisement further says: "You can have it too!" "Sign me up!" I say.

But God is not mentioned in any of this. God said He would provide us with an Abundant Life. Eve gambled away life and God for something that was "pleasing to her eye" and contrary to God's Word. Our culture promotes this same substitution today. A popular minister tells Christians they should not be satisfied with what they have, but should always want more. God wants His people to have more riches and He stands by to give them to us, he says. But there is a serious flaw to this reasoning: riches cannot take man from death to life. A God-connected emptiness cannot be filled by a "thing-connected" purchase. As we shall see later, the connection between "things," "riches," "worldly accomplishments" and "success" are very neatly tied into our culture's understanding and promotion of "living the American Dream." But God gives life; nothing else can.

Self-Confidence Is the Answer

But maybe the problem is something else. Maybe it is self-esteem. If we had greater self-esteem and self-confidence perhaps then that "hole" would go away. A word search of "self-confidence" in the Amazon book section discloses an amazing 74,755 entries, a strong indication that self-confidence and self-esteem issues are of great concern to huge numbers of people. A sampling of the titles: (1) *The Ultimate Secrets of Total Self-Confidence*; (2) *The Confidence Plan: How to Build a Stronger You*; (3) 30 *Minutes to Self Confidence + How to Be Assertive...and Well Liked (Super Strength)*.

I would like to obtain "super strength" in thirty minutes and would love to have "total self-confidence." But I have my doubts. Others are skeptical too, concluding that lacking self-confidence is part of the human makeup. Audrey Hepburn once stated:

> I lack self-confidence. I don't know whether I shall ever get it. Perhaps it is better to be unsure of yourself as I am. But it is very tiring. My epithet will be, "It's nerves what done her in."

As for her Hollywood success, she said:

> I don't think your insecurity ever disappears. Sometimes I think the more successful you become, the less secure you feel. This is kind of frightening really. [Melissa Hellstern, *The Audrey Hepburn Way of Life, How to be Lovely*, pages 38–39. Penguin Group (USA) Inc.]

She is right. Self has real limits. We cannot understand, perceive and face every "bend in the road of life." We walk around in bodies susceptible to injury and disease. We make decisions from an intellect that stems from a brain constructed out of dust, and that to dust will one day return. Our bodies and emotions cry out to the fragility of our being and to the multiplicity of unanswered questions about life's most basic questions. We live in a universe of billions of galaxies and planets that are a mystery to us; we have relationships that often baffle us; an unmarked future worries us. Our days are numbered, and we don't know the number. We look to the sky in wonder, reduced to a speck by its eternal massiveness. None of this is a confidence builder in the power of self, is it?

God Is Spirit

"The Spirit gives life." (Jn 6:63)

Man Is of the Flesh

"The flesh counts for nothing." (Jn 6:63)

The above circle illustrates the problem with self-confidence as the answer to "filling the hole." God is at the top of the circle. He is Spirit. "The Spirit gives life." We are at the bottom of the circle, of the flesh. "The flesh counts for nothing" (Jn 6:63). Accordingly, more confidence in self, the flesh, is not the solution. We *are* the problem, not the solution. Being of the flesh, we are inherently unable to fill the hole of our own inner being. The missing link is God who gives life, and greater self-confidence in our abilities cannot give us God. Our "flesh counts for nothing" in its ability to be God, or to supply God. God is our missing inner link: "*[He]* may strengthen you with power through His Spirit in your inner being" (Eph. 3:16). Indeed, it was Eve's self-confidence that led us into our mess in the first place.

Eve had great self-confidence, leading her to disobey God and to conclude by the power of her own reasoning that the forbidden fruit was good for her life, that she would not surely die if she ate it. She self-confidently concluded that she knew more than God. She was wrong. Self-confidence did not lead her to a better life. It destroyed her, and it destroyed us too, her children.

So it is not greater confidence in self we need to direct our lives, but greater faith in God, who has said: "I will instruct you and teach you in the way you should go. I will counsel you and watch over you" (Psalm 32:8). And while the Bible does not state that we need to exercise greater self-confidence, it manifestly states that we need to exercise greater self-control, for our nature is inclined toward sin and subject to self-destruction: "Like a city whose walls are broken down is a man who lacks self-control" (Prov. 25:28). "For the grace of God that brings salvation has appeared to all men. It teaches us to say 'No' to ungodliness and worldly passions, and to live self-controlled, upright and godly lives in this present age" (Titus 2:11–12).

In her book, *Surviving Myself*, actress Jennifer O'Neill writes about how she accidentally inflicted herself with a gunshot wound. While phoning to get medical assistance, her mind raced, thinking about the spiritual disorder that had led to her latest tragedy:

> By instinct, my mind sought escape from my body's pain. I tried to ponder the bigger picture like the good little New Ager I was in those days. I realized I had blasted my way through life in a whirlwind of extreme behavior, foolish relationships, and horrifying, if not predictable consequences. I had given God no real authority so far because I was convinced that I was in the driver's seat. But now I hoped, and somehow believed, He would grant me a reprieve. Mostly I realized how terribly I'd spun out of control. My life was a maelstrom. While this

> latest and most horrific instance of chaos and destruction had not been caused by my hand, all the choices that led up to this moment were mine. I had filled my dance card with some pretty twisted characters and now the day of reckoning was upon me.

Faced with the decision of going on with life, she said:

> The previous year of my life had pressed every alarm button I knew I had, and some I couldn't have imagined. A raging debate erupted between my heart, mind, and soul as to whether I just wanted to let it all go. Staying alive had become increasingly less attractive with every new disappointment. I struck a wary bargain with myself; I vaguely remember deciding at least to enjoy my time under anesthesia, to exist in limbo between life and death. At least I'd have a short break from the stress and sadness that had been sapping my energy for years. That seemed marginally preferable to my old strategy: "when in doubt, regress." [Jennifer O'Neill, *Surviving Myself* at 189, 190, 191. William Morrow and Company, Inc. 1999, 1st ed.]

The Price of Pride

Faith promotes God. Pride promotes self. Perversely, our "American Dream" culture promotes those "pumped up with pride," the "stars" of our American culture. But God did not create us to be a "star." He created us to be a servant, in the image of His Son. Lucifer is the Bible's example of the "star," the fallen angel who was thrown out of heaven because he fell so in love with himself he wanted to be like God and to be worshipped as though he were God (Isa. 14:12–14).

America's "star-studded" culture mimics Satan's character, with its vanity, envy, selfish ambition and promotion of self. God warns about the danger of this kind of thinking: "For where *you find envy and selfish ambition,* there you will find disorder and every evil practice" (James 3:16). The actress Tuesday Weld was a victim of Hollywood's "star making machinery," leading to more than one suicide attempt. When asked by an interviewer what caused her to "crash off life's road," she flippantly replied, "I think it was a Buick." Life without God is a "crash course" in living. Expect massive road damage if life without God is your self-confidently selected course for living.

"Fill it up please?" Nothing of this world can "fill up" up a dead man to make him alive. In the following chapters, we will see some of the worldly ways people seek to "fill it up," why they make the choices they do and why having a goal to "live the American Dream" is an extremely poor choice that can lead to deadly consequences.

God/Life

The hole fillers: More "things" to fill the hole;
Greater self-confidence to fill the hole.
*Result: Hole remains—something **big** is missing*

Tune In, Turn On, and Drop Out

The year was 1967 and I was a senior at the University of California at Berkeley. The culture had changed dramatically since I was a freshman. Walking down the street, I saw the cover story on one of the nation's premier news magazines, "Is God dead?" But the cover story had it all wrong. God wasn't dead—man was dead, and this could be abundantly seen in the culture.

God and Satan are in opposition to one another. What God proposes, Satan opposes. If God's presence creates a peace that passes human understanding, Satan's presence creates a disorder that passes human understanding. If God's Spirit works to transform His children into the image of God, Satan works to transform man into the satanic image: wickedness, sinfulness, perversity, rebellion against God. The satanic message is always the reverse of God's.

The sixties brought with it the Hippie movement, one of the strangest movements in American culture. Fed up with the stiff and materialistic culture of the fifties, many of my generation were now seeking the opposite. One should "do one's own thing" and "loosen up, man!" The generational mantra was "tune in, turn on and drop out," a recipe for living from Timothy Leary, a professor of chemistry at Harvard, who discovered LSD, a mind-altering drug that turned many on, off and out for good. "Far out!" as they used to say. Indeed it was.

San Francisco was the gathering place for the Hippie movement. *If you're going to San Francisco be sure to wear some flowers in your hair*, a best selling song of the "flower child" era advised. It was a colorful and pleasing message, although completely nonsensical: (1) go to a place; (2) with a flower; (3) put it in your hair; and (4) you will find peace and love. Really?

By my senior year, many of the "flower children" had drifted over the Bay Bridge into Berkeley near the University, crowding the city sidewalks. As I walked down Telegraph Avenue after class, I now had to pick my way among aimless youth, many obviously "strung out" on drugs. Some wore "flowers in their hair," but the flowers rested wilted and askew on unwashed and unkempt hair. The message of "love" was really an excuse for "free sex," resulting in unwanted pregnancies, broken homes, drug addiction and a poverty of body, mind and spirit. On the Berkeley campus, one student organization was the "Sexual Freedom League."

One night in a small restaurant, finishing my meal, I left pizza on my plate. As I left, a young person rushed over to eat the scraps. I felt disgusted and ashamed that so many of my generation were spinning so badly out of control. The lost generation of the sixties had forsaken God and turned to a lifestyle that was morally decadent. In meeting one another, we would sometimes give the "peace sign." But nice gestures could not disguise what was underneath. The stirring of the human heart was still man without God, and a peace sign can't quell a heart at war.

The sixties culture was aptly described in Ephesians 4:18–19:

> They are darkened in their understanding and separated from the life of God because of the ignorance that is in them due to the hardening of their hearts. Having lost all sensitivity, they have given themselves over to sensuality, so as to indulge in every kind of impurity, with a continual lust for more.

I saw all of the above. And the foregoing could be stated as an epitaph for many living in the drug-soaked sixties. Peer pressure was intense to do what everyone else was doing, to: "let go," "be free," "open up one's mind," "make love." Nice expressions. Terrible consequences. Peace is a Person: "Peace *I* will give you," Jesus said. Having rejected Christ, the "flower children" swerved right to left, left to right, looking for the latest fad that promised an answer to being, direction, peace.

One night at an off-campus event, the Maharishi Mahesh, who had received publicity for being the religious guru of the Beatles, came to Berkeley to impart his wisdom to those who, like myself, were searching for spiritual truths. He was a little man, bearded and dressed in white clothing. He entered the stage, sat down, folded his legs, and smiled. After some silence he spoke. He said things long since forgotten, but words that left me disappointed by their triteness, leaving me with the distinct impression that I had been "taken" for the price of an admission ticket. So, back into the night I went, wondering if there was anything in this world that could be believed.

Yet, spiritual devastation can come in a commune or in a mansion. The devil is not dependent upon a particular place in which to spread his disease. He is looking for any person whose mind is fertile to his worldly suggestions. The vulnerable may be the druggie on a street corner, or a person whose goal is completely focused on career, success and getting ahead.

Many of the "flower children" would soon reverse course completely, tired of their flower painted Volkswagens, sandals and beads. Soon the Beatles would split up, the music would change, and the Vietnam War would end. Many were weary of the confrontations, the riots, the peace marches. They wanted something entirely different. They wanted lots of money to purchase an expensive car and to move to a lovely suburb. Some of the "flower children" would become "soccer moms" and some of the dads would become successful business executives.

Those without Christ are described in Ephesians 4:14 as being: "infants, tossed back and forth by the waves, and blown here and there by every wind of teaching and by the cunning and craftiness of men in their deceitful scheming." This aptly describes the journey of those lost in the sixties. Having swerved in one radical direction in a search of meaning and finding no answer, they would now swerve to the opposite direction, right back into the arms of the American Dream.

God/Life

The hole filler: sex, drugs, rock n' roll; "freedom"
Result: hole empty—something ***big*** *still missing*

Shop til You Drop — Greed Is Good

Time ushers in new trends, fads and living styles. In the sixties it was "sex, love and rock and roll," flower painted Volkswagens, communes, long hair, beads, incense, and bell bottom trousers. By the seventies, a best-selling book was *Winning through Intimidation*. By the eighties, "greed is good" had become an anthem of the decade, taken from Gordon Gekko, a corporate raider who gave a speech in the 1987 movie *Wall Street* to corporate stockholders:

> The point is, ladies and gentleman, that greed, for lack of a better word, is good. Greed is right, greed works. Greed clarifies, cuts through, and captures the essence of the evolutionary spirit. Greed, in all of its forms; greed for life, for money, for love, knowledge has marked the upward surge of mankind.

The Prosperity Train

In the eighties, the high tech industry was birthed for many Americans, changing the way business, schools and individuals worked, played and communicated. High tech stocks exploded to the upside, and people threw money into them, hoping to catch instant prosperity. Investment returns soared, price/earnings ratios went into the stratosphere, and happy investors spent their money with vigor. While the answers had shifted radically from those of the sixties, at the core they were fundamentally the same. Sensing that something inside was missing, man still sought "completion."

Satan will supply this "completion" to fit the generational need, whether it be a sixties mind-altering drug, or a twenty-first century steroid. He will provide his misdirection in a commune or in a mansion. His "fruit" is: (1) outer; (2) of this world; (3) pleasing to the eye; (4) temporal; (5) in need of constant replacement; and, (6) it never provides a spiritual understanding of life, or proper direction about how to cope with that gnawing inner sense of "incompleteness."

Buying into the American Dream

The seventies was an exciting time to be in Washington, D.C. The city vibrated with headlines of antiwar protests, Watergate scandal and news from the Vietnam War. Soon, an administration would topple, a President resign, and persons holding high-level jobs in the Nixon administration would be indicted and go to jail. In the city attorney's office where I worked, my colleagues and I would discuss these events, and we would share our "war stories" of courtroom litigation and office intrigue, not seeing the intrigue that was taking place right under our noses.

Near the end of the work day, the division supervisor would drop a bundle of traffic violations he had reviewed on our desks, telling us to "no paper" the tickets, a technical term for dropping the charges. We would do so, placing the appropriate notations on the tickets, which would then be forwarded to the Violations Bureau to be taken off the computer.

We did not know that our supervisor was dismissing traffic citations in exchange for money and favors. He later became a judge and, either through blackmail or greed, continued this activity while on the bench. Once discovered, he was indicted on felony charges, pled guilty and served time in jail, dying several years later a broken and dishonored man. He was a Christian.

A facet of Satan's world is that one never has enough things in life, so we want more money to buy more things to get more happiness and to get that ever illusive "richer life" that will make us a "success." After all, there is so much to buy and so little time.

The temptations to spend are all around us. I can walk into a department store perfectly satisfied with my life and possessions. But in a matter of minutes, the colorful shirts and jackets, the nice furniture and the pretty colors and dashing displays begin to peck away at my "inner need button." I am lucky if I can escape without purchasing "some little something" to give color to my life, to satisfy that important need I didn't know I had before entering the store. Purchasing more and more beautiful things is an important part of the American Dream, for our material possessions testify to others about our "success in life."

A famous movie star during an interview was lamenting to a reporter about how his actress wife had a neurotic absorption to shop constantly for new things. Just as he said this the door opened, and in she walked with many bags of new purchases. "There!" he said. "See what I mean! It never stops!" Not too much later, the couple divorced.

Stores have many slogans to fortify and encourage our need to spend, to get us in on those very important "deals of a lifetime." We can shop at a "Midnight Madness Sale," at a "Pre holiday Price Slash Sale," at a "Back to School Sale," at a "Huge Savings! January Clearance Sale." We can shop at the "End of Winter Sale," "End of Spring Sale," and "End of Summer Sale." It goes on and on.

The Addiction

While these marketing blitzkriegs certainly boost retail sales, they also promote "shoppers' addiction," an unhealthy spiritual neuroses that leads the unsuspecting to believe that a new purchase is just a "life-changing moment away." The same elements discussed before are present here: (1) a person senses something missing in life; (2) he or she reaches out for more and more things to fill the hole; (3) the more one gets, the greater the frustration; for no matter how many things are purchased, the hole remains, so more must be bought if the "hole" is to be filled. The shopping addiction is handed down from parent to child, friend to friend, a perverse form of "consumer evangelism." We don't need a flu shot in this culture—we need an anti-shopping shot.

Many get so caught up in this web of shopping and buying they do not see the problem or what it is doing to their lives. Our American Dream culture insidiously plants the "bug" that creates the illness, neatly tying "success" and "completeness as a person" to filling our lives with things, the more abundant and more expensive the better.

Magazines encourage us with their pictorials of Hollywood stars who dress glamorously. We are informed about who is the "best dressed" (the "successful star") and who is the "worst dressed" (the "failure"). Because we want to be a success too, we mimic what we see. So why not get that radically new perfume, only $100 a bottle, designed to get you to smell like a success and to help you get the man or woman of your choice? I open a magazine and a perfume aroma floats from the page into my nostrils, coats my fingers with fragrance, lures me into the fantasy of that better life only a $100 purchase away. My dog comes over, sniffs the page and walks away, snorting. He has far better judgment than I.

We love those miracle lotions and liquids that promise to make us look better, smell better, be seen as better. People stand in long lines to see glamorous stars, to touch them and to get their autograph. If we can just see them, touch them, dress like them, live like them, smell like them—then maybe we can be like them!

The Touch

All the devil needs to get us to "touch him" for this "better life" is a credit card and a misconceived notion of spiritual reality. On the news today, it was reported that a riot broke out at a Virginia department store during the Christmas season as customers fought over a new toy in nationwide short supply. Police had to break up the disruption, firing pepper spray into the crowd. One man is shown in a photo with a sneer on his face, holding up this newly purchased item. The devil must delight in such tragically misguided thinking that leads people to fight over a toy during the Christmas season. I can assure you there was no crazed massing of people wanting to purchase a Bible that day. Police did not have to pepper spray crowds at a Bible store to get customers to behave.

It is not the touch of a toy that provides life with healing, but the touch of Jesus. The blind, disabled and demonically possessed cried out that He, Jesus, "touched me," "healed me," "cured me," "gave me sight!" "Once I was blind, now I see!" Healing comes from God, not from a purchase at a Midnight Madness Sale. A more beautiful life is not just another glamorous purchase away. Satan knows this, so he wants us to partake of *his* worldly "touch," not Christ's touch. God instructs us to be content with what we have, that it is better to give than to receive. The satanic lie is exactly the opposite, that we are never to be content with what we have, that we are to want more and more. Greed is good. Spend yourself silly. Go ahead—you deserve it! As the quote at the beginning of this chapter said:

"Greed, in all of its forms; greed for life, for money, for love, knowledge has marked the upward surge of mankind."

It is the inability to discern the nature of the illness that leads so many to the wrong cure—that a good day of shopping, followed by many more, will fill an empty life. The American Dream puts life into the treadmill of wanting to move onward, upward and outward, informing us that with vigor and hard work we can acquire that magical American Dream purchase, the apple of every person's eye that will make us complete. Yet, do we stop to consider what the apple did to Eve?

God/Life

The hole filler: greed is good; prosperity; glamour; "shop til you drop"
Result: hole empty—something ***big*** *still missing.*

How Many Dead Things Do You Have?

One cannot pick up a magazine or a newspaper without seeing how to live the American Dream. For example, one must dress for success. Mark Twain once said he never knew a naked man who got anywhere in life. So department store catalogues point us to the things we need to keep us abreast of popular trends—how to "dress comfortably and fashionably for winter," "summer and fall"; "to dress successfully for business"; "to travel elegantly"; to drive the "right car" that will allow us to meet the "right guy," "gal," "business contacts." This kind of thinking begins early in life, for kids are very attuned to what others are wearing in school, the latest hair style, the proper length of one's pants. "Is denim in this year?" "Yes, it is!" "What a relief!" I say. After all, clothes make the man. God has little to do with it.

Proof of Success

As adults, the need and reasons to buy don't go away but expand, for one must not only have the right clothes but the right car. The more expensive the car, the greater the showing of business achievement. One must live in the right neighborhood. The more expensive the house, the greater the showing of "success." The house must be decorated with the right furniture, the more expensive the better. One must hire an interior decorator and be aware which decorator has the "right look" and the "important clientele."

People are also classified by whom they know. So, it is very important to have the right contacts who can provide further contacts who can be used to establish better contacts. Jesus did not have the "right contacts," and this enraged the Pharisees. "Isn't this person from Nazareth?" they said. "Who does He think He is, telling us what is right, what is wrong? This fellow walks and talks and dines with sinners!"

But Jesus boiled things down to very simple levels. It is not the appearance or possession of things on the outside that matters, but the condition of one's heart on the inside that matters. The worldly message is quite the opposite—the outside matters, so you must do whatever is needed to get more and more, for material abundance will establish your importance in life and give you great self-worth. "Here," the world says, "buy this object, so very pleasing to your eye. $3,000 a month, easy installment terms, set to fit any budget!"

My dog, Scotty, does not have a bank account, but I consider him to be very precious and important. He is lucky he is not a man for then I might have to consider him a failure because of the penniless state he lives in. Yet, Scotty has a very good sense of his self-worth. He doesn't have a dime but he is as happy as can be. In many ways, his logic is keener than mine. He is satisfied with little, and rejoices in life's simple pleasures. He loves his morning run, an occasional swim in a creek and the joy of sniffing through a heavily scented forest. He loves to explore the backyard and to have his evening meal, which he gulps down with great relish and a burp. He lives a simple life and has the wisdom to enjoy it fully.

Man does not like simplicity for it is far too easy and far too attainable. This will not do. So, one must prove himself through complexity. The mark of the successful person is the ability to "empire build," to get more money to buy more things, to turn a simple house into a technologically wired monstrosity, with a five-car garage, occupied by vehicles with complex and wonderful gadgetry. The more complex a person's moneymaking schemes, and the greater the return, the greater the showing of one's brilliance. Complexity makes the person. God has nothing to do with it. Yet, one can get so caught up in this treadmill of constantly purchasing, acquiring, scheming and dreaming that one can lose contact with the meaning of it all.

The Lack of Meaning

I enjoy the prints on my wall at home and the comfortable furniture in my house. I enjoy the colors that perk up the rooms, but all of these things are quite literally dead. They are also temporal and, in time, will wear out and need to be replaced. They cannot speak to me, counsel me, lead my life or give me lasting peace. They cannot wash away my sin. They won't be with me until the end of time.

Yet, the world has managed to pass off the American Dream in a most remarkable way, which if broken down to its most elemental form conveys the complete nonsense of its meaning. It goes something like this: (1) he who makes the most money can then (2) buy more things, and if one gets richer, then (3) he can buy many expensive things, and, (4) while all of these things are also dead, they are "expensively dead," and, (5) an abundance of "expensively dead things" demonstrates great success to others, who (6) don't have as many "expensively dead things," so, (7) he who has the most "expensively dead" things is living the American Dream and is (8) a success, while (9) those who do not have an abundance of "expensively dead things" are (10) failures.

Makes perfect sense, right? As a bumper sticker once said: "He who dies with the most toys wins." There is nothing in scripture to suggest that any of this impresses God. There is no confirmation anywhere in scripture that any of this is how one should live or direct his life. Yet, people direct their lives by this nonsense daily, and this includes many Christians. People need to meditate daily on Luke 12:15: "Be on your guard against all kinds of greed; a man's life does not consist in the abundance of his possessions."

Christian Prosperity

When I was in law school I lived in a garage apartment that leased for $35 a month. When the owner started his car in the morning, the exhaust would rush into the apartment through the cracks in the boarding, chasing me out of bed and out the door. My living quarters were only slightly bigger than the size of the bathroom in my present house. But looking back, I am basically the same person I was then. While the house in which I now live is far more expensive than $35 a month, the temple in which the Holy Spirit dwells—in my heart—has not changed. I would be stupid to conclude that, as a Christian, I can move from one end of town to the other and that this will substantively change the quality of my life. The richness of my life is not connected to where I live, but to Whom lives in me, and to how well I listen to His Presence, and to how well I ignore the teachings of a store catalogue. If this truth were communicated to the public by our nation's billion dollar marketing industry, retail sales would plummet to a sixty-year-low.

Does this mean a Christian must not want and must never purchase expensive things? Certainly not. But the Christian must keep biblical perspective about what is taking place. It is not our relationship to a "thing" that empowers our Christian life, but our relationship to God. The Christian walk is linked to God's voice, not the world's. "Do not let this Book of the Law depart from your mouth; meditate on it day and night, so that you may be careful to do everything written in it. *Then you will be prosperous and successful*," Joshua 1:8 says. Prosperity is the reward of the righteous, Proverbs informs us (Proverbs 13:21).

Thus, it is not a "thing-filled" life but a God-filled life that provides prosperity, regardless of the size of our bank account. For the heart to stay spiritually healthy, we may have to put aside the shopping list to buy more in order to expand the Christ list to give more.

Not surprisingly, the world never communicates this message for it has no interest in doing so. It wants us to keep chugging away at getting that American Dream: buying, planning to buy, planning to add, working ourselves silly to get more expensively dead things that will give us a little satisfaction and a greater desire to get something else that will give us an even greater satisfaction.

So, how many dead and expensive things do you have? How many more do you want? Why do you want them? When will you get enough?

God/Life

Hole filler: Abundance of expensively dead things
*Result: Hole empty—something **big** still missing*

Career Is Life

Not long after becoming a Christian, I was invited to the house of a prominent U.S. Senator, a Christian, a man who had written several Christian books. He greeted us at the door. He was a handsome man, dressed casually in his cashmere sweater and expensive loafers. We sat in his beautifully decorated living room, surrounded by wonderful artwork, nestled by the warmth of the crackling logs in his elegant fireplace. He shared with us the importance of faith in his life, his work and projects. He invited our questions and answered with polish, intelligence and diplomacy. I left his house thinking this man had everything, if only I could be like him. Not too much later he was censored by the Senate for unethical business dealings. A few years later, he was censored again for the same conduct, being at that time, the only Senator censored twice for such conduct. He was a Christian. He was gullible. So are we.

We live in a "career conscious" culture, one in which career, position and personal ambition are determinants of personal success. A component of the American Dream is not just "having much," but also "being much." Scripture tells us something completely different, that we are "complete in Christ" (Col. 2:10, NKJV), that personal fulfillment comes from our position in Christ, not from our position in the world.

Satan tempted Christ with worldly promises, offering Him position, power and prestige, a ludicrous temptation since, as God, Jesus already had dominion and power over everything in heaven and earth, including Satan. Christ indwells the Christian. So if we have Christ in our lives—directing, counseling and comforting—what can the world offer to make us more complete? After all, in Christ all things are held together (Col. 1:17), including you and me.

Yet, if the mindset is not on Christ but on the world, it is easy to forget this and to get spiritually off-track. The world's approval of a person is grounded on a slippery slope, in which human value must be proven time and time again. So it is very important to be viewed as a person of "power and consequence," a "major player," "one to be reckoned with" and not just for a short period of time, but forever. But this kind of mindset can be a poison. The Senator had power and great wealth but believed he needed more, even if it meant violating ethical principles. If our goal is to gain great power and position, we may find we have to compromise Christ, cut a spiritual corner here and there, to gain greater worldly prominence. But Christ cannot be compromised. Satan was a "murderer from the beginning" (Jn 8:44), and he delights not only in seeing a Christian fail, but in seeing a Christian destroyed.

After a few years, I moved from the litigation division of the city attorney's office to its appellate division. The new job was a very tough one, requiring an ability to research the law, write legal briefs, argue cases in appeals courts and handle a very heavy and complex case load in a very timely fashion. A colleague in the division, Perry, was transferred out of the division because he was unable to keep up with these demands. He viewed the transfer as a demotion, feeling his abilities as a person and as an attorney had been demeaned.

He did poorly at the division he was transferred to, still bitter over his reassignment so, under pressure, he eventually quit to take a legal position in a Maryland law office. He was fired from that job, after locking himself behind his door one day, refusing to meet with a supervisor. About a year later, I was walking down a crowded sidewalk in downtown D.C. when I heard someone call my name. I looked up to see Perry and was shocked by his appearance. He had just come from a job interview and said he had decided to leave the legal profession to go into sales. I thought to myself that no one would hire him. His collar was askew and dirty, his necktie dirty, his teeth were a dark yellow, his hair was long and unkempt. He said the last year had been a very rough one, and he mentioned his hurt in being transferred out of the division. His career "set back" had sowed a seed that was eating away at his mind, and his appearance and demeanor were evidence of this.

Another year passed and someone encountered him panhandling on a sidewalk. Several months later I got a phone call from my former secretary, asking, "Dennis, are you coming with us to Perry's funeral today?"

"What?!" I exclaimed.

"Oh, you haven't heard" she said. "Perry committed suicide. He jumped off the Key Bridge a few days ago." Perry was not a Christian.

Perry sensed his hole of "incompleteness" and concluded that a respectable career as an attorney would fill that hole. But it wasn't "career advancement" that would fill the hole. The hole was not of this world. The hole was the absence of God in Perry's life. Having misdiagnosed the disease, Perry sought the wrong cure. With his worldly "cure" gone, his life was destroyed, not worth living, he concluded.

This painful story is one I have thought about many times. A job will not make us complete. Without Christ, no matter how satisfying the job, the feeling of being "incomplete" will remain. The Christian life is a God-centered life, not a career-centered life. Jobs will come and go, but Christ is with us until the end of time. A job that ends for a Christian simply opens up another road, a new direction for God to lead us down. "I am the Lord, the God of all mankind, is anything too hard for me?" (Jer. 32:27). It is our position in Christ that establishes our "completeness" as an individual, not our position in the world.

Had Perry achieved great career success he still would have found his "incompleteness" gnawing away at him. James Forestal was an advisor to a succession of U.S. Presidents. He took great pride that so many presidents sought his counsel on important governmental matters, year after year, decade after decade. But one day a president was elected who did not want his advice. This was a crushing blow to Forestal and his mental condition began to deteriorate, eventually getting so bad he was placed in a hospital for observation and care. One day he opened the hospital window and jumped to his death below.

An aide to a former U.S. President told a similar story of how he found himself on the "outs" with the President. When this happened he began to doubt his abilities, to worry about his position and about what others were thinking and saying about him. Each morning he would walk swiftly to the front office to check the President's daily calendar, to see if he was being included in any of the meetings. His continued exclusion caused his mental anguish to grow, and it started to affect him physically. His face broke out in a bad rash and his hair began to thin. He eventually resigned and went to a Christian retreat to regain his bearings. He turned to a study of the scriptures and to prayer. In time he recovered and good health returned. But for him to get "spiritually ahead," he had to take a "career step backward," deciding to leave an "American Dream" job behind, serving the President of the United States. This was a decision that may have saved his life.

The world and its job-related demands will not provide peace to our heart, for our job is of the world and not exempt from giving us worldly troubles. Indeed, the wise have the discernment to understand that some jobs need to end, even if it means throwing away an American Dream. A friend of mine worked in the White House and the pressures were so intense she had a bad stroke, leaving her in speech therapy for years.

Proverbs 14:30 provides us with direction to steer us away from dangers like this: "A heart at peace gives life to the body." Dissecting the foregoing verse: (1) we need to examine our heart to see if it is at peace; (2) if it is not, then we need to see if our body is in good health; (3) if both heart and body are flashing danger signals, then (4) we may need to step back, or get away completely, from what is taking peace from our heart, so that life to the body can be restored. During my career I turned down several promotions, concluding that more pay and greater responsibility would not be a healthy experience for me as a person. I never regretted the decision.

Kim Novak, a movie star in the fifties and sixties, came to a similar conclusion. In an interview, she once shared about the compromises one had to make for "stardom," the harmful effect that continuing her career would have on her life and on her self-esteem, the moral compromises she would have to make to stay in a film career. One day, at the height of her career, she put all of her possessions in a station wagon and left Hollywood behind, moving far away. She was still young, still beautiful—a person who had made a name for herself—but it didn't matter. To stay, she concluded, would have been to be destroyed. She bought a ranch, eventually married a veterinarian, whom she is still married to many decades later. One of her regrets, she said, was that she did not sit down with her friend, Marilyn Monroe, and share her concerns. Marilyn died a few years later, from an overdose of prescription drugs, having stated to a friend a few days before that her movie career was over, her life destroyed. She was thirty-six-years-of-age.

Our walk with Christ is not a walk with the world. We are not to love anything in the world (I Jn 2:15), so giving up something of the world is not a calamity. Sometimes it is a necessity to give up an "American Dream."

God/Life

The hole filler: Success in job; career
Result: Hole empty; something ***big*** *is still missing*

How Far can You Run, Kick and Throw?

Some people use a "ball" to measure the "mark of a man" or the potential of a boy to become a "man." The ball can be a baseball, basketball, football, golf ball, etc. Any object that is speechless, that bounces and that can fly through the air once it is hit or thrown will do. If the ball could think, it would find it very odd that it has assumed such great importance to an entire culture and to cultures in other nations of the world. But important it is. Indeed, people will fight, gloat, smirk and measure their very self-worth over whether their team, their boy, their girl, their city wins an award for kicking, bowling, putting, shooting, hitting and/or throwing a ball better than someone else. Indicators of self-worth are contained in a "box score," providing statistics of who scored the most, who was in the game the most, who pitched the best. Students at some universities determine whether their university is "better" than another by the outcome of an athletic contest, and some are willing to fight about this after the game too, just to prove their point.

Many fathers aspire for their sons to be a superior ballplayer, linking manliness and individual worth to good ball playing ability. And some become very irrational about this. When I was in Little League, a pitcher on my team, Jim, was often berated by his father, Ted, who was our team manager. Ted wanted his son to be a major league ballplayer. If Jim threw a bad pitch, Ted would yell: "Jim, why did you do that!?"

Jim would answer: "I don't know! Leave me alone!"

"Don't tell me to leave you alone!" Ted would reply. Sometimes Ted would throw his hat on the ground, jump on it and scream at his son.

One day a batter hit a long fly ball into left-center field, and the fireworks began: "Why did you do that?!" said Ted.

"It's not my fault!" said Jim.

"Don't tell me that," said Ted. The fans were so interested in the father/son dramatics that most did not see my early jump on the ball, that I was closing in quickly on what had looked like an impossible catch. I raced and raced, thinking: "Don't worry, Jim. I will bail you out!" And I did, leaping into the air at the last moment, hauling the ball into my glove, the ball clinging to the glove's top webbing.

"Dennis caught it! Dennis caught it!" yelled the assistant manager. The crowd roared.

Ted looked up, saw the ball in my glove, and then said: "What?! eh? Oh?" And then: "Okay, Jim, just settle down now." Settle down? Jim? Now? Similar scenes would be repeated like this all season.

Jim never forgot that catch. My .012 batting average on the team didn't matter. My catch did. In high school he remembered me as that ten-year-old outfielder, making that spectacular catch, "bailing him out." He never made it to the majors and this created self-worth issues for him and his father, who fancied a "bubble gum" major league baseball career to settle all self-worth issues. Yet, Mickey Mantle was a huge major league success story and, shortly before his death, he related how he had been plagued all his life by feeling "unworthy," of something "missing inside." He spoke of how this led to problems with alcohol, problems in marriage and family life. A high school acquaintance committed suicide after he was dismissed from the Angel's organization. With no baseball career ahead, life seemed meaningless.

Athletic success is intertwined with being a super-strong person, one able to do more, to be more because of size, speed, strength, agility. Star athletes are perceived as "all-American boys," who marry the prettiest cheerleader, and who win the adulation of a community. But there is a darker side to this too. An athlete must get an "edge" over an opponent and be able to keep it for a very long time. Some try to do this through "performance enhancing drugs," for some will do "anything to win," anything to prolong a career. Drug use has become so prevalent in every major sport that routine drug testing is now common. Yet many athletes recognize the limitations of the human body, so they risk getting caught, thinking that getting and maintaining a competitive edge is worth the risk.

Lyle Alzado was a fearsome lineman who played for the Oakland Raiders. He was big, strong and portrayed himself as the toughest of tough, a man to reckon with on and off the field. To enhance his strength, he took steroids, which he later blamed for the brain cancer that destroyed his body. Shown in an interview shortly before his death, he was a changed man, walking feebly with a cane, a bandanna wrapped around his head to hide his baldness, his body terribly shrunken in size. Speaking of his reputation as a fearsome football player, he said it was all an act, just a show, and that all he wanted to do now was just smell a flower. Several months later he died.

The roar of approval is an intoxicant to a professional athlete, for it rolls across a playing field like thunder, as thousands applaud that marvelous catch, that spectacular touchdown. But it is also temporal. Soon the applause stops, and the next play may be an error or a dropped pass, converting a supportive crowd into a disparaging one. And the "iron man" image of an athlete is often a very short one too, as age and injury bears down on the body. Lou Gherig, the "iron man of baseball," died from a muscle debilitating disease. Muhammad Ali, who "stung like a bee and floated like a butterfly," incurred brain damage so severe it destroyed his ability to communicate, a terrible price for "rope-a-doping" to another "ring victory." Jim Otto, all-star center for the Oakland Raiders, has shared of his post-football arthritic body pains, of the fifteen minutes or more it takes to put on his socks in the morning.

Larry Colton, who graduated from Berkeley several years before me, writes in his book *Goat Brothers* about the trials and tribulations of climbing baseball's ladder of success. Signed his senior year by the Philadelphia Phillies, he married the daughter of a well-known movie star. His baseball career followed, pitching for several years on minor league teams, riding from town to town on broken-down team buses, living in cheap motels, giving in to marital waywardness and other vices. Gradually he worked his way up to the major league club, where he pitched just a few innings in just one ball game. In a major league interview he said: "It's funny...The big leagues have been my goal since I was five. Then you get here and the novelty wears off in five days." [Larry Colton, *Goat Brothers*, page 304, Doubleday 1993, 1st edition]

His major league career was cut short by a debilitating shoulder injury incurred from being physically assaulted outside a restaurant. Back in the minors, his marriage dissolved; he found himself one of the oldest players on the team. Pondering the situation, he wrote:

> It was scary to think about quitting. *Baseball had been my life*. It was what *defined me*. I was a baseball player, then a husband, then a father. My adult life had been designed by my fastball, not my college diploma. Baseball *affected every decision* I made. I also believed baseball had influenced Denise's decision to marry me—if I was a shoe salesmen, no matter how good, she wouldn't have married me. Baseball was *glamorous, masculine, respected*. It offered the promise of *money, travel, adulation*. I didn't

> know anything else; I had *no other* career *frame of reference.* I had loved the game, the competition, the fraternity with the players. I loved standing on the mound being the *center of attention.* It was *power, control.* Its loss would be a *loss of self,* I worried. But I was ready to quit. (p. 352)

Notice the spiritual significance of the foregoing italicized words, their displacement of "baseball" for God.

1. "Baseball had been my life."

But baseball is not life. Jesus is life: "*I* am the way and the truth and the *life*," Jesus said (Jn. 14:6).

2. Baseball "*defined me.*"

A "sport" does not "define us." *God defines us.* God created us, and instructs, teaches and provides in the way we should go (Ps 32:8).

3. *Baseball was glamorous, masculine and respected*, promising *money, travel and adulation.*

It was this same "pleasing to the eye" kind of temptation that lured Eve into sin and that leads us into sin today. Here Colton's enticements were: a) glamour; b) masculinity; c) respect; d) money; e) travel; and, f) adulation. Yet, God has us focus on the opposites: "What does God require of you? To act *justly* and to love *mercy* and to walk *humbly* with your God" (Micah 6:8). And adulation?—"God opposes the proud but gives grace to the humble" (James 4:6).

4. Baseball was "*power*" and "*control*" and to lose baseball was to "*lose self.*"

The Bible says something starkly different, that "in him *all* things hold together" (Col. 1:17), and of course this includes baseball. Yes, if baseball is life, then once baseball is gone, life is lost, as Colton experienced.

These are hard lessons for our culture to learn. The bleachers are filled with parents, including Christian parents, who envy the athlete signed to a professional contract. We vicariously think of the good life in store for this "super athlete," "winning one for the Gipper." We fancy the "All American" life of riches bound to come his way: the "glamour," "respect," "money," "travel," "adulation." But Jesus is "life." A life without Jesus is a life that will go awry, major league contracts aside. Colton's baseball career did not lead to the American Dream success story he had envisioned. He described the aftermath this way:

> I was thirty-seven, supposedly prime time for a man to hit financial and emotional maturity. Instead, I had two ex-wives, two ex-careers and an oxidized old Nova with a broken transmission. Its only gear was reverse. (p. 465)

The American Dream can throw life into reverse, with its credulous fixation on sports as the answer for the good life. A friend of mine, a former quarterback in the NFL, described the doldrums he went through after his career. He was depressed because his football career had been short and disappointing; horrified at the prospect of looking for a "real job" with no education or training to assist him, and disgusted he had let football so completely define his reason for living and the way he chose to live. He is a Christian.

I turn on the television on the weekend and find much of the airtime connected to a sports event. Some fans sit in the stadium with their shirts off in twenty degree weather, their bodies smeared with grease paint. I see a doctor's appointment in their future. I have seen the lives of Christian men and women turn bitter for days if a favorite team loses, if a son does not "measure up," as though going 0–5 in a Little League game is a "life changing event," jeopardizing the boy's future, calling the boy's masculinity into question. There is a spiritual malaise that accompanies this kind of thinking, that self-worth is connected to the bounce of a ball. Satan must delight in the complete illogic of this, rejoicing in his ability to destroy so many lives, in so many ways, by a cultural displacement of God by a piece of rubber.

God/Life

*The Filler: Athletic success; professional sports contract; marries cheerleader; adulation of fans. Result: Hole empty; Something **big** is still missing.*

Going Up?

I walked out of my office after a busy morning in the law library, doing legal research, writing an appellate brief, struggling to keep up with an overwhelming work load. I strolled over to the newspaper vending machine at the corner of 14th and Constitution, one block from the White House, thinking with pleasure about the foot-long coney, smeared with mustard and onions, I would soon purchase at my favorite deli. I lifted the newspaper out of the stand, closed the machine cover, took a step and was abruptly jerked back by something around my neck. Startled, I turned to see my neck tie caught in the cover of the vending machine. I yanked at the tie, but it would not come loose. I tried to take off my tie, but my neck was too close to the cover of the machine to do so. I reached in my pocket for a quarter to open the machine, but I was out of change. So there I stood on one of the busiest intersections in our Nation's Capital, an assistant city attorney, enslaved to a newspaper machine, and with no freedom in sight. I was helpless. Someone had to come along to release me, to set me free.

Fortunately my predicament lasted only a few seconds. A man came along, chuckled, put a coin in the machine, opened it, assuring me he had intended to buy a newspaper anyway. I am certain he had an amusing story to tell people once he got back to his office. As for me, my lips were sealed.

The Bottom of the Circle

Let us return to the circle:
God is Life

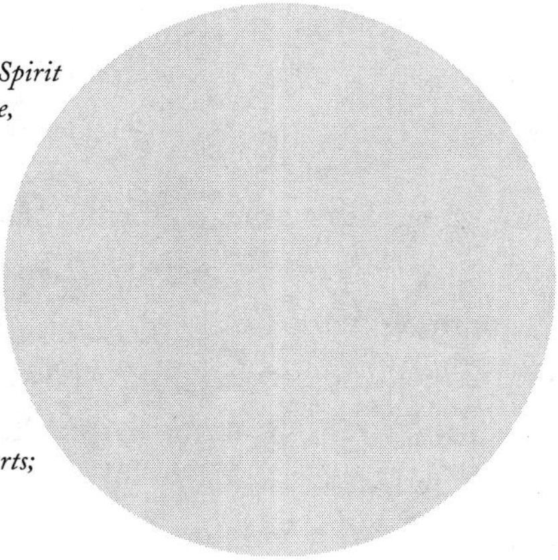

We can see the fix we are in, trapped at the bottom of the circle, spiritually dead in our trespasses and sins. The Bible refers to the bottom of the circle as "the dominion of darkness" (Col 1:13). Following the circle from top to bottom, we see: (1) the Holy Spirit is breathed into Adam and Eve, giving man life; (2) God warns Eve that "*when*" she eats of the forbidden fruit she will die; (3) Eve sins; the Holy Spirit, who gives life (Jn 6:63), departs; (4) man is left "dead in [his] trespasses and sins" (Eph. 2:1), a body without the Spirit; and, (5) this condition is handed down to us: "Surely I was sinful at birth, sinful from the time my mother conceived me" (Ps. 51:5).

In my newspaper example, the newspaper machine was holding me in bondage and I needed someone to set me free. In the spiritual context, it is "sin" that holds us in bondage, for we are born "prisoners of sin." We need someone to set us, the captives, free. We want to go from the bottom of the circle, death, to the top of the circle, life. But who will take us, and how?

The Choice

"God's elevator" stops at our residency at the bottom of the circle. The door opens and we hear these glorious words: "Going up?" Notice the choice. Many love the darkness and have no desire to leave it for, to a wayward heart, the freedom to sin provides the misconceived "cherished opportunity" to disobey God, to live by one's own rules, as though one is God. These people will decline God's invitation to "go up," choosing "to stay down."

But a remnant will choose to "go up." "Only the remnant will be saved" (Rom. 9:27). Their response to God's invitation will be fast and furious: "Yes!" they say, "please, take us up! Get us out of here! Fill us up God! We have tried everything!"

And indeed by this time we will have tried everything. We will have "shopped til we dropped"; burned ourselves up with long hours at the job; attained a successful career at the cost of a few nervous breakdowns; filled our house with expensively dead things. We will have chased the American Dream, and we have the evidence to prove it: an overly mortgaged home; 2.9 spoiled children; a lavishly expensive car, now in the shop with a two thousand dollar repair bill. Our life is entangled with financial woes from trying to "keep up with those exasperating Joneses." Some will have tried sex, drugs and rock n' roll as long-haired hippies; pitched in the major leagues; achieved "sports star status"; earned lots of money, spent lots of money. Nothing: the infernal hole remains and sin plagues us, dampening our spirit, taking away our joy. What to do?

The problem is that a dead man can't do anything: dead men can't walk, talk, breathe. A dead man at the bottom of our circle is in a grave, which is why he is called "*dead* in [his] trespasses and sins" (Eph. 2:1). Sin is the problem. Sin led us from life to death on the left-side of the circle and it keeps us in a grave at the bottom of the circle.

But if death came quickly with man's choice to turn away from God, life can come quickly with a man's choice to return to God. With the fall: (1) sin separated us from God; (2) the Holy Spirit departed our lives; and (3) the "hole," God's absence, entered our being. With Christ it is all reversed: (1) His blood cleanses our sin; (2) the Holy Spirit indwells us; and (3) we are reconciled with the Father. The fall came as quickly as the bite of an apple; salvation comes as quickly as a heartfelt prayer to receive Jesus. In my newspaper example, a stranger put a coin in a slot to deliver me from bondage. In our spiritual life, Christ put Himself on a cross to deliver us from bondage. "For *he* has rescued us *from the dominion of darkness* and *brought us into the Kingdom of the Son* he loves" (Col. 1:13).

Notice how the circle has changed:
Spiritually alive: A body with the Spirit

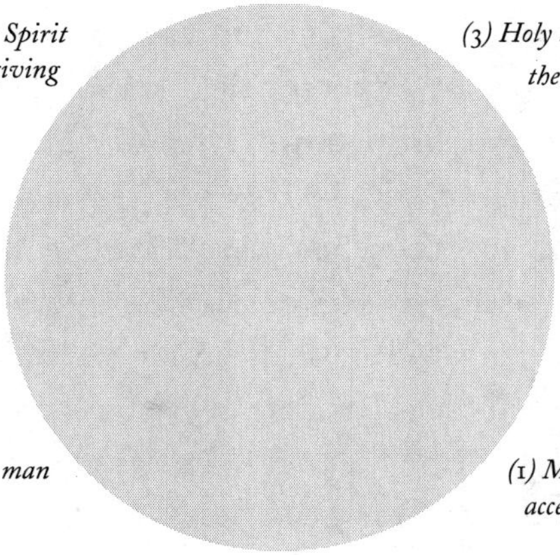

The Filling:

With sin washed away, our body now becomes the temple of the Holy Spirit: "Do you not know that your body is a temple of the Holy Spirit, who is in you, whom you have received from God?" (1 Cor. 6:19). Hence, the filling of the hole is internal, filled by God, who lives in us and who makes us complete.

Notice some parallels regarding our spiritual journey: (1) it was man's choice that took him down; it is man's choice that takes him up; (2) it was Christ who gave us life; it is Christ who gives us new life; (3) it was the devil who tempted man into sin and a life without God; it is the devil who does the same today; (4) it was God who created us to be in His image; it is the indwelling Holy Spirit who now works to transform us into God's image; (5) it was idol worship that took us down; it is the rejection of idol worship that takes us up; and, (6) it was grace that gave man life before his fall; it is grace that gives man new life after the fall.

But what about the American Dream? The formulas of the American Dream are of the world, those "baseball is life" worldly fillings on the left side of the circle that served as idols, a substitute for God, promising us a full tank and leaving us with a tank empty. It is choosing God's Word on the right side of the circle that took us to life. But many Christians will forget their journey or be ignorant of the message of their journey or be ignorant of where their journey has actually taken them. So they will still engage in left-sided circle wanderings, trying to fill up a hole that has already been filled, caught up in worldly American Dream ambitions they still believe must be achieved if they are to live prosperously, be successful, live "the good life." These are Christians lost in the American Dream, living on the wrong side of the circle.

Lost in the American Dream

Money Honey

An old Elvis Presley song called "Money Honey" went something like this:

> I screamed and I hollered I was so hard pressed,
> I called the woman that I loved the best,
>
> I finally got my baby 'bout half past three.
> She said I'd like to know what ya want with me?
>
> She said, Money Honey,
> Ya gotta have Money Honey,
>
> Money Honey,
> if ya wanta get 'long with me.

The lyrics remind us that money sets the standard for getting along with some people. We have heard the expressions before: "Money Talks"; "Hey, Big Spender!"; "I've Got The Time If You've Got The Dime." The slogans put dollar quantification on human value, telling us which persons deserve attention, which persons don't.

Money Buys

Money buys: things, attention, power and, according to the Presley song, some form of "love" from some kinds of people. Money is cherished for its value, but is also widely known for its vaporizing properties. It can be overspent, stopped with a "pink slip," robbed at gunpoint, and disappear with a bad investment. Money has no sound, no voice and is a very dull companion to be with, but people will kill to get money for the things it provides. The things money buys are speechless and temporal. Money cannot buy wisdom, understanding or love. Money dwells on the left-side of the circle, the very side of the circle that took us from life to death. God is on the right-side of the circle, the very side of the circle that took us from death to life. It is thus bewildering that, having been saved by the right side of the circle, the left side of the circle becomes for many Christians the focus of attention for living a "successful life." Yet the Bible tells us not to love the world, so the world should not direct our lives.

Not of the World

We are in the world, but not of it, Jesus said (Jn 17:14). When we took "God's elevator up," He took us from the world's bottom floor, and death, to the top floor, and life, for God now indwells us. "Lord you have been our dwelling place" (Ps. 90:1). Because Christians are not "of this world," our calling is an "out of this world" communication from God, who has made us citizens of heaven (Phil 3:20) and "aliens and strangers in the world" (1 Pet. 2:11).

In the Garden of Eden, God provided life for Eve, but she accepted the devil's lie that a "pretty thing" should be believed over God. "Here: take, eat," Satan in effect said to Eve. The American Dream incorporates this same lie, portraying wealth, things, power, position as the embodiment for a "successful life." "Here: take, eat," the world says. This is what led to man's fall in the first place, the substitution of things for God.

The left side of the circle is the "life-taker." The right side of the circle is the "life-giver." The materialistic components for a "good life" are consolidated into the American Dream and expressed by its system for judging human worth: "How much do you have?" "Who do you know?" "How good are your prospects?" "Where do you live?" "What do you drive?" "How high is your position?" "What are your accomplishments?" etc.

By American Dream standards, Jesus Christ was a total failure: an unemployed thirty-three-year-old carpenter; born in a barn; who dined with sinners; who had no schooling; who came from the wrong part of town; who died penniless; who was forsaken by His friends; who died on a criminal's cross. None of this was "pleasing to the eye" of the world, or measured up to American Dream "successful life" standards, but all of this was pleasing to God: "You are My Son, whom I love, with you I am well pleased" (Luke 3:22). Jesus Christ does not conform in any way to the tenets of the American Dream.

For this reason, what pleases God will differ radically from what pleases the world. And we can see why: (1) The world tells man he is empty and must continuously prove himself or fall from favor; God tells the Christian he is "complete in Christ"; (2) the world tells man he must make a name for himself; God tells the Christian to rejoice that his name is written in heaven (Luke 10:20); (3) the world tells man that he must strive for success and that financial and material rewards will fill the inner hole; God tells us our inner hole is spiritual and can only be filled and is filled by the indwelling Spirit of God; (4) the world sends man out to "make more," "get more," "be more"; God sends the Christian out to be "Christ's ambassadors" (2 Cor. 5:20), to share the gospel message to the lost; (5) the world tells man that worldly treasures will reward our lives; God tells us our rewards will be given in heaven, based on how we have built our lives on the foundation of Christ (1 Cor. 3:12–13). While no points will be given for having lived the American Dream, they will be given for having lived as a servant of Christ (1 Cor. 3:14).

Still Dancing with the American Dream

When we were at the bottom of the circle, "God's elevator" stopped and its attendant asked, "Going up?" But now that we are at the top of the circle, alive with God, Satan's elevator will stop and his attendant will ask, "Going down?" Many Christians will go down, concluding that the worldly principles for living the American Dream still apply. But the Bible says something completely different: "Since you died with Christ to the basic principles of the world, why, as though you still belonged to it, do you submit to its rules…" (Col. 2:20).

Although saved, a Christian is still subject to temptation. The world still presents its glittering array of things and people to distract us from our calling, things that tempt our eyes and arouse our senses, and that we are around every day. But the Holy Spirit now dwells in our hearts and He is not voiceless. God speaks. "But you know him for he lives with you and will be in you" (Jn 14:17). And because He dwells within us, speaks to us, shapes our inner being, we now see differently, hear differently, act differently than the world. Christ gives us spiritual sight and hearing, but of course we must still open our eyes to see, our ears to hear. "Surely you desire truth in the inner parts; you teach me wisdom in the inmost place" (Ps. 51:6). So God's voice bubbles up from within, like living streams of water, nourishing us, cleansing us, healing us and leading us to still waters that provide quality to life, regardless of our how many things we own, how much money we have, or what our worldly title is.

It is the substitution of the American Dream as the giver of life, for God as Giver of Life, that converts the American Dream into a nightmare, leaving houses filled with things, hearts cold and empty, souls separated from God, people left in dire confusion over life's meaning. In a recent *Newsweek* interview, Sylvester Stallone observed:

> You see billionaires who have everything, yet inside they're still the same lonely, insecure people. You think you've got it all figured out, but then you turn 60 and there's still this little hole inside you. You realize, we're always going to be somewhat half full. [Sylvester Stallone, *Newsweek* interview, pg. 74, Dec 18, 2006]

I recall a very rich man in my hometown who had everything the world could provide but who was sadly lacking in wisdom and understanding about the very life he lived. I recall a very poor man who polished shoes for a living at our local shopping mall, who spoke with such wisdom and insight about life that to this day I remember his Christian witness. The poor man found God, acted on His Word, and prospered in the richness of God's wisdom and inner provision. The rich man gave his life to living the American Dream, substituted it for God, and was impoverished by a spiritual hole the American Dream promised to fill but couldn't.

Eve rejected the Word of God and fell; we opened our ears to the Word of God and rose. It is nonsensical to conclude that, having risen, we are now to live our Christian life on the side of the circle that caused us to fall. We need to examine our lives daily, search our hearts, for it is a Christian tragedy to be lost in the American Dream.

What You Say?

We all need direction in life, and direction is provided by some form of communication. I go on a road trip several times a year and rely on a map to point me and keep me in the right direction. But if the map is faulty, providing bad information, I will end up far from where I want to be. If the map says turn right, I must turn right; left, I must turn left.

In the Garden of Eden, Adam and Eve were given direction by God on how to direct their lives, that they were free to eat from any tree in the garden, but they must not eat from the tree of the knowledge of good and evil, that "when you eat of it you will surely die" (Gen. 2:16–17). This was the roadmap from God, providing "direction" on what to do, what not to do, where to go, where not to go.

The Misdirection

Satan excels in providing misdirection. He is crafty (Gen. 3:1), "there is no truth in him," "a liar and the father of lies" and a "murderer from the beginning" (Jn 8:44), who was cast out of heaven when he rebelled against God (Isa. 14:12). In Heaven, he misdirected other angels to participate in his rebellion, and they were thrown out of heaven for having tried. So Satan's design was not to nurture Adam and Eve whom God created in His image, but to get back at God by destroying His creation, converting Adam and Eve from God's image into Satan's image, and he knew exactly how to do it.

First, he would disparage God's Word, substituting his own words, changing "You will surely die" (Gen. 2:17) into "You will *not* surely die" (Gen. 3:4). In Revelation, God provides this warning to those who change His Word: "if anyone adds anything to them, God will add to him the plagues described in this book. And if anyone takes words away from this book of prophecy, God will take away from him his share in the tree of life and in the holy city, which are described in this book" (Rev. 22:18–19).

Next, Satan masqueraded as an angel of light (2 Cor. 11:14), making poisoned fruit look pretty, nourishing and the source of wisdom, rather than the passage to death it really was. Satan's design was to insult God, to get Eve to exchange the Word of God for the "wisdom of an apple": "When the woman saw that the fruit of the tree was *good for food and pleasing to the eye*, and also *desirable for gaining wisdom*, she took some and ate it" (Gen. 3:6). Three components leading to man's sin were: (1) changing God's Word; (2) masking evil as pretty ("beauty") and nourishing ("food"); and (3) convincing Eve that wisdom lies outside the Word of God.

Lost Communication

When Adam and Eve sinned and the Holy Spirit departed their inner being, it was not just the inner presence of God that was now absent, but also the inner voice of God that was now absent. Having chosen Satan over God, man would now be directed by satanic communication on how to live. God distanced Himself from man, becoming remote, an ominous presence: in a burning bush; a fiery cloud; behind a curtain in the "Most Holy Place" of the tabernacle (Heb. 9:3). His laws were written coldly, impersonally on tablets of stone. Satan had promised that by rejecting God's Word, man would live "like God." "Your eyes will be opened and you will be *like* God," he said (Gen. 3:5). God gave man centuries to prove Satan's promise a reality. The Israelites believed that, even without God's Spirit within them, they could of their own flesh live Holy lives. God said:

> Now if you obey me *fully* and keep My covenant, then out of all nations you will be my treasured possession. Although the whole earth is mine, you will be for me a kingdom of priests and a holy nation. These are the words you are to speak to the Israelites. So Moses went back and summoned the elders of the people and set before them *all* the words the Lord had commanded him to speak. The people all responded together: "We will do *everything* the Lord has said." So Moses brought their answer back to the Lord. (Ex. 19:5–8)

But the Israelites did not do everything the Lord said. They disobeyed all of His laws. After King Solomon's death, the nation of Israel split into two kingdoms, a Northern Kingdom, called Israel, and a Southern Kingdom, called Judah. Both nations disintegrated into great wickedness. The people of both nations were warned repeatedly about their evil practices, including idol worship, practicing occultism and child sacrifice. With respect to the Northern Kingdom, Israel, God said:

> They forsook *all the commands* of the Lord their God and made for themselves two idols cast in the shape of calves, and an Asherah pole. They bowed down to all the starry hosts and they worshiped Baal. They sacrificed their sons and daughters in the fire. They practiced divination and sorcery and sold themselves to do evil in the eyes of the Lord, provoking him to anger. (2 Kgs 17:16–17)

With respect to the Southern Kingdom, Judah, God said:

> The people of Judah have done evil in my eyes, declares the Lord. They have set up their detestable idols in the house that bears my Name and have defiled it. They have built the high places of Topheth in the valley of Ben Hinnon to burn their sons and daughters in the fire—something I did not command, nor did it enter my mind. (Jer. 7:30–31)

> They built high places for Baal in the Valley of Ben Hinnom to sacrifice their sons and daughters to Molech, though I never commanded, nor did it enter my mind, that they should do such a detestable thing and so make Judah sin. (Jer. 32:35)

In Judah, witches used charms and mystical rites to cast spells and attempt to tell fortunes (Ezk 13:18–19). God punished His people for their persistent rebellion against His Law, eventually permitting the Assyrians to overrun Israel and Babylon to overrun Judah.

Under the Control of the Flesh

Man without the indwelling Spirit of God became Godless in thinking and conduct. "It's no use. We will continue with our own plans; each of us will follow the stubbornness of his evil heart" (Jer. 18:12). Satan's objectives were achieved: (1) man created in the image of God was now converted into the image of Satan, the ruler of the world; (2) inner, personal communication between man and God had been destroyed; (3) the sinful mind was now set on whatever the sinful nature desired (Rom. 8:5).

The American Dream is a product of the sinful nature, directing man away from God to "idols of the heart," things, aspirations, pleasures idolized as having the ability to make life complete, with no reference to God; hence: (1) "success" is correlated with material riches and career achievement, with no reference to God's view; (2) lifeless treasures of the world "give life," not God: "The words I have spoken to you are spirit and *they are* life" (Jn 6:63); and, (3) "living the American Dream" becomes an idol, misdirecting people away from God to an American Dream "success story" in which God sits on the bench, a substitute player for our empowerment.

A random look at this week's television shows, with the recitation of their content from the television log: (1) *Deal or No Deal*: "A resident of Santa Claus, Ind, competes for $1 million." (2) 1 *vs* 100: "A holiday-themed mob stands between a contestant and cash." (3) *Show Me the Money*: "A junior ROTC instructor plays for more than $1 million." We live in a "money-mad" culture in which "Show Me the Money," rather than "Show Me God's Word," has become our cultural mantra.

The Code Breaker

If communication between man and God was destroyed from the outside by Satan, that communication would now be restored from the inside by God. With Christ's death: (1) sin is washed away; (2) the Father remembers the Christian's sin no more; (3) the Holy Spirit dwells on the Christian's heart; allowing (4) communication between God and His people to be restored. One cannot receive Jesus without receiving the Voice of Jesus. Jesus made this clear: "My sheep listen to my voice; I know them, and they follow me" (Jn 10:27). To the Jews, God promised that "***if*** *they obeyed God fully*" and kept His covenant, then they would be His "*treasured possession*" "a *kingdom of priests*" and a "*holy nation*" (Ex. 19:5). As seen, the Israelites not only did not obey God fully, they forsook "*all the commands* of the Lord" (2 Kings 17:16). What the Israelites were unable to accomplish by works, the Christian has had accomplished by grace, as Christ's blood washes away all of the believer's sins, placing the Christian as the beneficiary of God's promise: "But you [Christian] are *a chosen people*, a *royal priesthood*, a *holy nation*" (1 Pet. 2:9).

Christ's salvation power and indwelling spirit now decodes for us the devil's lies. Just as Satan reversed God's truth by adding to and deleting the Word of God, God has now responded in kind, reversing Satan's lies. "We have not received the spirit of the world, but the Spirit who is from God, that we may understand what God has freely given us" (1 Cor. 2:12).

God's voice speaks to our heart, elucidating our inner being, enabling us to unravel thoughts, mannerisms, habits and sins that have entangled our lives through years of worldly bombardment. "The lamp of the Lord searches the spirit of a man, it searches out his inmost being" (Prov. 20:27).

I had just seen the movie *The Exorcist* and I walked away dumb struck, horrified by its message. Could Satan be real, Christ be real? So one night I prayed: "God, I am going to take one crack at this. If you are real, I want you to disclose yourself to me, show me that Jesus Christ is real." For weeks I read books on how the Bible was written, searched for evidence that Christ lived, died, rose from the dead. I met with a pastor at a church, who gave me the Book of John and told me to read it. At about 3:00 a.m. one morning, with the evidence piling up, I pounded the side of my chair, saying: "I can't believe it! Christ is true! Christ is real!" A week later I met with my pastor, who scheduled my baptism for the following Sunday morning. As I walked up to the church that morning, I prayed that God would give me the strength at my baptism to answer the pastor's questions not in a whispery voice but with power. As I knelt in front of the church to receive Christ, his first question was: "Dennis, who is your Lord and Savior?" I opened my mouth to speak normally, but my voice bellowed: "*Jesus Christ is my*

Lord and Savior!" I spoke so loudly, the pastor lost his place in the text. I jokingly told friends later, "They could have heard me at the gasoline station across the street."

Communication had been restored. And this restoration continues for all Christians as we look to the world with spiritual eyes and ears that allow us to see and hear anew the world in which we live. I look at the television programming each night as an alien, turning off the set, disgusted by program after program of sex and violence, and "game shows" in which contestants, with wild looks in their eyes, grovel over the opportunity to get "rich."

Our worldly culture immerses us with "road maps" that have set our nation off course with God. "This is what the Lord says: 'Stand at the crossroads and look; ask for the ancient paths, ask where the good way is, and walk in it, and you will find rest for your souls'" (Jer. 6:16).

But at that crossroads, Satan also stands with a different road map, saying turn to the left while God has said turn to the right, for Satan remains the master of deceit, relishing the destroyed lives his misdirection conceives. It is Christmas day as I write this, and I have just accessed the internet. On the AOL home page, the question is asked: "What did *Santa* bring to you this Christmas day?" I rest my case.

How Much Brick and Mortar Do You Have?

As we have seen, man got lost by losing communication with God and by accepting communication from Satan. But the satanic reach does not stop at misdirecting a person, it is also designed to misdirect a church. The Church is the body of Christ, the witness to the world. The world is not supposed to be the witness to the Church, or the Church the embodiment of the world.

The American Dream is a crafty one, for it is so splendid in appearance, wealthy in presentation, and it attracts such beautiful looking people as "success stories" that churches can get caught up in the American Dream message, thinking I want my congregation to look like that, to be successful, attractive, wealthy. Some prominent pastors are promoting the message that Christians should aspire for worldly success, that they should make more and more money, have goals to live in elegant homes, travel first-class, for "success" is a sign of God's favor on a Christian's life. But who defined "success" in this way, God or the world?

Satan destroyed the "inner of man" by means of the "outer of the world," importing a word here and deleting a Word there to "clarify God's message." Once the satanic communication was accepted over God's, that very communication destroyed man's character, conceived by God to be Holy, but now poisoned by Satan so we would be a prisoner of sin. (Gal. 3:22)

As Christians, we are the chosen people of God (1 Pet. 2:9), but the satanic attack on us and the Church takes place in the very same way: (1) Take the Word of God out; (2) put the worldly in;

and (3) bit by bit the inside gets corrupted, for "a little yeast works through the whole batch of dough" (Gal 5:9).

I recall reading several years ago about a pastor in a large church in Texas who said he did not like to mention the word "sin" to his congregation for fear it would make people uncomfortable. A church I belonged to out east had to leave its presbytery after the presbytery sanctioned the ordination of those who rejected Jesus as the Son of God. These are obvious transgressions that will destroy a church, and Satan is becoming more successful with these all the time.

But there is also an "American Dream displacement" taking place that is spiritually disemboweling churches. Like men, churches can get enamored with size, a critical American Dream component for measuring success. Size matters much to our "size conscious" culture. The bigger the house and the larger the salary the more successful the man. By this American Dream reasoning: the bigger the church and the larger the donations the more successful the church. "Successful pastors" are those with the largest congregations, with the largest building programs, with the largest media exposure.

Some churches compete for attention on the basis of building programs, how much "brick and mortar" is being put into place, going up, being planned. Some churches get so enamored with brick and mortar they don't know when to stop, a prayer tower here, a basketball court there, an indoor running track here, regardless of spiritual need or budgetary realities. Solomon built his temple lavishly but it had nothing to do with the spiritual health of what resulted, becoming more a witness to the ego of man than to the glory of God. We cannot fool God by brick and mortar, by enormous fundraising drives, by worldly media coverage, for "the Lord does not look at the things man looks at. Man looks at the outward appearance but the Lord looks at the heart" (1 Sam. 16:9). God will not look kindly on a lavishly constructed church, filled with Christians who have the opportunity to play basketball in a church gymnasium, run on a church track, but be free from hearing about sin on Sunday mornings because it might make them uncomfortable. God allowed Solomon's temple to be destroyed, replacing it with His temple on the believer's heart, which cost us nothing and His Son everything. Solomon's temple was not allowed to stand, for while it was beautiful on the outside, it had become spiritually corrupt on the inside.

A little bit of worldly yeast can go far in destroying church thinking, direction, purpose and witness, for worldly focused activities bring with them worldly attitudes. Is a win by the church basketball team a sign of God's blessing? A loss, a sign of God's disfavor? If the church athletic program is languishing is it a sign the church is languishing? Does "winning one for the Gipper" subtly displace winning a soul for Christ? The competitive spirit of the worldly can be yeast that infects a church, destroying its unity, undermining Christian witness.

Paul would be amazed by the effort of many churches to make their people more comfortable, for Paul's ministry cannot be represented as a comfortable one. Paul was shipwrecked, beaten, jailed, scorned and executed for sharing the gospel. The devil delights in seeing more of the world in a church, less of Christ.

Jesus did not have a large building to preach in, or a large budget or the best of disciples: twelve disciples, one a traitor who stole from the treasury and who conspired to kill Him; another who doubted His resurrection presence. This was a poor record for Jesus, one likely to receive disparaging reviews from the popular ministers of His day. On the other hand, the Pharisees had a very good record: healthy attendance at their places of worship; great personal prosperity too, with their fancy robes, political following and access to the top rulers of the day. They were very successful in their business of religion, with a healthy market place for bringing in great amounts of money. Jesus was not impressed by this, taking a whip and driving the money changers from the temple, saying their activity was an abomination in the eyes of His Father.

Jesus talked about things that made people uncomfortable. Indeed, most of what He said made people uncomfortable, things about: the wealthy, our love for money, the need to look after the poor, the trappings of the world, the presence of evil, the lying of Satan, the corruption of the clergy. Most of what He said would cast living the American Dream in an uncomfortable light. It is Satan who likes to make the church comfortable and Jesus who does the opposite.

Jesus did not cater to the politically almighty of His day for He knew too well His Father Almighty. His appearances were not highly staged church events. There was not a chariot race, a gladiator contest or a sports event that has ever been recorded in conjunction with His teachings. He fed the needy, talked to the outcast, comforted the lonely, and confirmed His divinity by raising the dead, giving sight to the blind, driving out demons, seeing and rebuking Satan and then rising from the dead Himself. The people came, followed, learned and the church grew, robustly. The Word of God was enough to reach the heart of man. The Word has not changed, nor has the power of Christ, who "is the same yesterday and today and forever" (Heb. 13:8).

There is an "American Dream embedded fear" that has crept into many churches today saying that if a church is not big enough, wealthy enough, comfortable enough, on television or radio enough—then it is not successful enough and may lose to "the competition." But God worked mightily when people had too little: David had a slingshot; Abraham followed, not knowing where he was going; Joseph prospered from a prison; Moses stuttered and had little self-confidence and would have been dismal on radio or television. None of these people evidenced signs of being part of an American Dream success story, but they are giants of our faith.

The comfortable church of the American Dream needs to be careful. For with the worldly comfort that finds its way into a church may also come the worldly yeast to sour the Bread of Life. The church cannot serve two masters, the world and Jesus.

So how big is your church building program, how much brick and mortar is going up, what is coming in and what is going out, what is being gained and what is being lost? Is your church lost in the American Dream?

Something for Nothing?

The Communication

We turn on the radio in the morning to get the latest news and are greeted by the "state of the economy." The dollar is up or down; oil prices are over $60; home construction is down; it is a home buyer's or seller's market; industrial productivity has risen by .3%, stunning analysts who expected a .1% rise; interest rates are rising, bad news; interest rates are falling, good news; but not expected to continue to decline, bad news; the Fed is concerned about higher inflation, bad news; but "prosperity is right around the corner," good news, or so the politicians tell us, bad news.

Our morning stop at the gas pump is greeted by a twenty-cent rise in the price of gas and the grocery store is passing along its higher food prices because of a persistent drought. At the office, we are informed that company sales are in decline due to greater competition from other companies. We have learned all of this in the first two hours of the morning and then the wife phones to say she "just must go" to the "Midnight Madness Sale" at the mall, that the bank has not phoned about refinancing the mortgage and that the Joneses, across the street, just bought a beautiful new, lavishly equipped Mercedes SUV that gets ten miles to the gallon. Shouldn't we keep up with the Joneses? We are besieged by callers who want our donation to their worthy cause and who will give us a lapel pin as a token of their appreciation.

In short, "money talk" saturates a good portion of our day, enveloping our mind with whether our life is turning the right corner or falling off a cliff, or perhaps both. If someone offers us something for nothing, our mind instantly clicks into "What's the catch?" and "What's it really going to cost me?" Nothing worth anything is given for free, and we also know that quality things cost lots of money. Nothing good in life is free. Or is it?

The Problem

"Getting ahead" in life is a very costly experience for it requires being able to understand a baffling array of personal and market indicators that will enable us to know when to buy, when to sell, how to grow our investments. Investing incorrectly can result in calamitous results that may throw a family's balance sheet into red ink, ruin a business and roil our "peace of mind." Our aim is "peace of mind" and lots of money can give it to us, along with greater success, a higher standard of living, a better quality of life and maybe an affirmation from a pastor who believes God is rewarding us for our moneymaking abilities.

So in the world, personal well-being gets insidiously connected to the bounce of the dollar, a bad bounce and our peace of mind tanks; a good bounce and we are exuberant. Love springs from a mindset on something that makes us happy, makes us feel good. Love provides us with a sense of direction, purpose and completion as a person. But a fixation on money can quickly be morphed into a "love of money," which according to God is "a root of all kinds of evil" (1 Tim. 6:10). Rather than loving money we are supposed to: "Love the Lord your God with all your heart and with all your soul and with all your mind" (Matt. 22:37). In our "show me the money" culture, with its consistently positive encouragement of American Dream aspirations, it is easy for a heart and soul to wander from love of God to love of money, even for Christians.

The Price of Peace

But the dollar-focused heart and mind seldom rest in peace, for as the fortune of the dollar bounces from good to bad, so too does inner peace. The American Dream is focused on getting more, having more, enjoying more, believing that "more" will provide more of everything that is good in life. But disappointment can come strongly when the money is going in the wrong direction, when money outflow drains money inflow, leaving a desert to our dreams and a blow to our ego. If we want to have peace and good in this life, we must pay for it, for nothing comes cheap and nothing of value is freely given—so we gotta make the dough, Joe!

Internals versus Externals

As we have seen earlier, however, the "inner hole" is a spiritual one, not "thing-connected" but "God-connected." We cannot buy God. And because God *is* Peace, we cannot buy peace. If we leave God out of the equation, we leave inner peace out of the equation. The worldly provision of "peace" and God's provision of peace are very different: (1) worldly peace is temporal, rising and falling with our emotional well-being; God is eternal, all-powerful, all-seeing, able to calm our inner storms; (2) the world's provision is always exterior, unable to reach the heart; God's peace is on the heart: God "set his seal of ownership on us, and put his Spirit in our hearts as a deposit guaranteeing what is to come" (2 Cor. 1:22); (3) worldly peace must be purchased; God's peace is a gift, given by grace, not by our works (Eph. 2:8); (4) worldly peace "warms over" our problems to temporarily make us "feel good" until another problem arises; God's peace is unaffected by the world's direction, for "in him all things hold together" (Col. 1:17), including our lives. And most importantly, peace is a person, Jesus Christ, not of this world, so His peace passes human understanding because of its spiritual ability to discern, touch and heal; a mere touch of His cloak has healed.

God Gives Freely

God gives to us freely in many ways. Our justification and redemption were given to us freely through Christ on the cross. We did not have to pay a penny for our salvation, and we will not have to pay a single coin to enter Heaven. Our names are already recorded in heaven. God "helps us in our weakness," as His Spirit "intercedes for us with groans that words cannot express" (Rom. 8:26). We do not pay for His intercession. Also Jesus stands at the right hand of God interceding for us (Rom. 8:34). We do not pay for this either. God's angels look after us: "Are not all angels ministering spirits sent to serve those who will inherit salvation?" (Heb. 1:14). This does not come at a financial cost to us. "Things" are also provided to us by God free of cost: "He who did not spare his own Son, but gave him for us all—how will He not also, along with him, graciously *give us all things*?" (Rom. 8:32).

Counseling services are free for the Christian, provided by the Holy Spirit who dwells in our heart, prays for our needs, and communicates to us spiritual truths needed for inner healing (1 Cor. 2:12–13). However, the worldly are charged a fee for the professional counseling they receive, but their worldly counselors cannot understand spiritually based problems: "the man without the Spirit does not accept the things that come from the Spirit of God for they are *foolishness to him* and he *cannot understand them* because they are spiritually discerned" (1 Cor. 2:14).

The American Dream takes a fierce grip on a person's life, telling a person if he wants "to be something," to "make a name for himself" and to "be successful" then he has to live up to rigorous American Dream standards that, if achieved, will win him the approval of men. Paul dismisses this as irrelevant and faulty thinking for a Christian: "Am I now trying to win the approval of men, or of God? Or am I trying to please men? If I were still trying to please men, I would not be a servant of Christ" (Gal. 1:10).

The foregoing punches a huge hole in American Dream reasoning, for if peace with self comes from peace with God, why "live for the American Dream" to obtain a peace it cannot give and for an American Dream lifestyle that has no message other than to "get ahead"? "What good will it be for a man if he gains the whole world, yet forfeits his soul?" (Matt. 16:26).

The truth has set us free, but we must have the spiritual acumen to understand the fullness of that message. The world "winds us up," churns our digestive juices into ulcers, coaxing us into worry about the latest economic indicators and the initiatives we must take in order to "get ahead in life." God tells us to relax, that inner peace is inextricably connected to Him, a peace the world has no ability to give: "Peace I leave with you; *my* peace I give you. *I do not give to you as the world gives*" (Jn 14:27).

None of the above means that we are to be lazy or idle. We are to work to the best of the ability God has given us, for laziness is contrary to God's design and not in the image of God. What we say, how we act and the manner in which we work are a witness to our faith and to those who are searching: "For we are to God the aroma of Christ among those who are being saved and to those who are perishing" (2 Cor. 2:15). But our faith changes our attitude about work and career from that of following the false shepherd of the American Dream to following our true Shepherd Jesus Christ.

In our work, Jesus may shepherd us to a high position with great power, but, as with Daniel, we will not have to blush over the way we got there. Once during an interview, I was asked how far I wanted to rise in the Solicitor's Office of the federal agency to which I was applying. I knew the answer that was expected, that

I should say I wanted to rise to the very top and would work very hard to get there, an affirmation of the drive and ambition they were looking for in a young attorney. Instead, I replied that I would work at 100% of my ability each day and that, if I did that, the future would take care of itself. There was a pause. The Associate Solicitor looked out the window, then back to me and said, "Good answer." I got the job.

Peace in our lives is not connected to following the American Dream but to following God's voice: "If only you had paid attention to My commands, your peace would have been like a river" (Isaiah 48:18).

God exposes our culture's "show me the money" mantra as a delusive "philosophy" of a fallen world communicated to us from its fallen angel, Satan, who can only be expected to miscast our purpose in life as having nothing to do with God. The biblical message is, of course, the opposite: We are not to lean on our own understanding, but in all of our ways to acknowledge God, and then He will make our paths straight (Prov. 3:5).

It is not the fountain of the American Dream we are to drink from with its heavily polluted waters. Rather God has said: "Whoever is thirsty, let him come; and whoever wishes, let him take the *free gift* of the water of life" (Rev. 22:17).

It is the devil's handiwork that leads man to choose that which is expensive, worldly and that provides nothing over that which is free, of God and that provides everything.

The Costs

It is expensive to live the American Dream, expensive for the individual to keep purchasing more "necessary items," to move into more expensive housing, to keep supplied with all of the "state of the art" technology and other things that will make lives more enjoyable, comfortable and successful. Living the American Dream is largely a self-focused activity, driven by the personal need to get ahead, stay ahead, not lag behind and be at least as comfortable as every other successful person.

Human Demand

The spiraling effect of this kind of mindset, once adopted by billions of persons in the world, can have alarming consequences. The energy supply for larger houses, more houses, bigger cars, more manufacturing must soar in order to meet far greater energy demand. America now imports 65% of its oil. In 2007, according to the investment firm Lehman Brothers, oil demand will be about 86.5 million barrels a day, a worldwide consumption rate of about 1,000 barrels of oil a second. The world is not discovering 1,000 barrels a second, or anywhere near that. China's oil demand alone is growing at a rate of about 500,000 barrels a day according to Lehman, and as more of its 1.2 billion people enter the middle class that demand will be far greater. Statistics from the U.S. Department of Energy show that in January of 1998 a barrel of oil cost $14.34; today, $63.10. The North American production basin for both oil and gas is now largely "picked over," with more rigs being required each year to produce the same amount produced the previous year. More greenhouse gases are pouring into the atmosphere, resulting in a global warming of the planet according to many scientists.

In its July 2006 report, the National Aeronautics and Space Administration stated:

> Global surface temperature has increased [approx] 0.2°C per decade in the past 30 years...Warming is larger in the Western Equatorial Pacific than in the Eastern Equatorial Pacific over the past century, and we suggest that the increased West East temperature gradient may have increased the likelihood of strong El Niños, such as those of 1983 and 1998. Comparison of measured sea surface temperatures in the Western Pacific with paleo-climate data suggests that this critical ocean region, and probably *the planet as a whole, is approximately as warm now as at the Holocene maximum and within [approx]1°C of the maximum temperature of the past million years. We conclude that global warming of more than [approx]* 1°*C, relative to* 2000, *will constitute dangerous climate change as judged from likely effects on sea level and extermination of species.* [National Aeronautics and Space Administration Goddard Institute for Space Studies, open access article, July 31, 2006]

God's Plan

When God created the earth, He did not intend for His ecosystem to be destroyed by the greed of man, and it is *His* ecosystem, not ours:

> Psalm 24:1, "The earth is the Lord's and everything in it, the world, and all who live in it; for he founded it upon the seas and established it upon the waters."
>
> Psalm 89:11, "The heavens are yours, and yours also the earth; you founded the world and all that is in it."
>
> Deuteronomy 10:14, "To the Lord your God belong the heavens, even the highest heavens, the earth and everything in it."

So God provided that man was to be a steward over the earth's creation which He created in love (Gen. 1:28). But a hardened and greedy heart will do anything, take anything to satisfy its need, regardless of how wanton that need might be. God has dealt with this kind of attitude before. The fall of Israel came during a time of great national prosperity, but also during a time when the greed of His people stirred God to anger:

> These Israelites were living in a time of renewed prosperity as Israel extended its borders. They poured their wealth into their homes, lavishly decorating them with expensive paneling and ivory carvings...However their opulence was too often paid for by defrauding the poor... For that reason, the Lord promised to foreclose on the proud Israelites' expensive real estate. There is a lesson here for rich Christians today. There may be nothing inherently wrong with owning two homes or furnishing them attractively. But God always pays attention to our treatment of others, especially the poor...It is a dangerous thing to lavish luxury on ourselves, particularly if we are doing so at the expense of others. We may find God not only "foreclosing" on our material lifestyle, but bringing us into a time of spiritual crisis as well. [*The*

Word in Life Study Bible New King James Version, page 1508, Thomas Nelson, Inc. 1993, 1996.]

Living the American Dream promotes a "theology of desire" that is way out of bounds with real need, that stimulates demand from the earth's finite resource base that may bring it to a point of exhaustion. As noted, we may already be seeing this with oil production. King Solomon contributed to the decimation of the forest of Lebanon in order to provide the lumber to build lavish palaces, resulting in the complete destruction of a massively large forest, so completely annihilated that it could never be replaced (See 1 Kings 7). We are intended to be the steward of the planet, not its exploiter (Gen. 1:28).

Many scientists believe man has initiated a mass extinction in the life of the earth. In general, they believe the following broad categories are contributing to this event:

> habitat destruction and fragmentation—the destruction or splitting up of once continuous habitat to enable humans to use the land for agriculture, development of towns and cities, construction of dams, or other purposes;
>
> climate change—human activities such as the burning of fossil fuels, have altered the Earth's atmosphere and have resulted in global climate changes;
>
> introduction of exotic species—accidental and intentional introduction of nonnative species into regions never before occupied by the species have resulted in the extinction of numerous endemic species;
>
> pollution—pollutants (pesticides, herbicides, etc.) released into the environment are ingested by a wide variety of organisms;

over-exploitation of resources—exploitation of wild populations for food has resulted in population crashes (overfishing, for example);

hunting, poaching, illegal trade of endangered species—some endangered species are targeted for their value on illegal markets.

[*Understanding the Threats to Animals and Wildlife*; www. About.Inc.com, A part of The New York Times Company, 2007]

Wildlife

Wildlife would be very puzzled by the activity of man. The animal gets up in the morning, looks into the distance, stretches, hungers for his meal, just as we do. They give birth to their young, look after them, nurture them, take pride in a first flight out of the nest. The animal has not built mansions during his time on earth, as we have. A hole, a nest somewhere will do. They cannot build expensive machinery to take them where they are going, as we have; they have not built expensive recreational resorts to make their lives more comfortable, as we have. They have not polluted the air, streams and waterways with chemical poisons, as we have. But they have become victims of all of man's predatory activity, as we have encroached upon or eliminated their housing, poisoned and killed their presence, so that we can be made American Dream comfortable by their absence.

The animal does not have an American Dream philosophy to guide him into becoming a more "successful being." He simply wants to eat, breathe and enjoy the time he has been given. The urbanization of our culture has resulted in an increasing number of people who are separated from wildlife and separated too from the "other worlds" of God's creation: His forests, rivers, oceans and His animals who inhabit each. As a result, man plows over, kills and cares little for that which is "out of sight" and "out of mind." God must not be pleased with what He is seeing.

The Christian Science Monitor recently observed:

> The World Conservation Union's "Red List" is at an all-time high: 16,119 threatened species (out of 15 million estimated species). This century-old trend is largely human-made and ongoing, with one harbinger being the extinction of many large mammals from North America. One mammal humans warm to, the polar bear, has now been joined with another huge environmental challenge: climate change. The US Fish and Wildlife Service is to rule any day on whether to propose listing the polar bear as endangered. Environmental groups such as the Center for Biological Diversity say global warming is melting the ice on which the bears live. Climate change is likely to raise awareness about species extinction. But what about concern for a creature as lowly as a shellfish? One way to bring remote plants and animals to the public consciousness is by connecting them with human life itself. A recent report in the journal Science had this effect when it estimated that 90 percent of the fish and shellfish species from the ocean that feed people worldwide may be gone by 2048.
>
> A powerful moral argument can also be made: Species deserve an opportunity to survive. [www.csmonitor.com; commentary, The Monitor's View, Dec. 21, 2006 edition]

Once a week I volunteer at the wildlife rehabilitation refuge in my neighboring town and see personal and up close these other creatures God loves. On one of my first outings, I saw a baby dove, as small as a man's forefinger, lying on a towel, shivering, its eyes in pain from some scourge inflicting its body. One of the animals at the refuge is an American kestrel, a small falcon, that was brought to the center by a person who saw the bird surrounded by several boys, kicking the injured bird, having already dug a hole for its grave. Now it sits in a nice cage, fed daily, looked after and nourished. You look at the beauty of this animal and it looks back at you, and you wonder if it wonders about you, remembers the cruelty of the human heart that once caused it so much pain.

The animals recognize their stewards, those who love them and care for them. Percy, a pelican, each evening waddles behind a familiar face who leads him to his place of shelter for the night, but if a strange face tries to do the same, he squawks and shows resistance, perhaps wondering who this person is and what he has in store for him. A small squirrel rests comfortably in the crook of a volunteer's finger, taking nourishment from a syringe, much like a human baby taking nourishment from a bottle.

These are creatures who do not operate as we do. If they are sick, they cannot phone for medical assistance. They have no money, no savings to fall back on in hard times. They never ask us for money if they are hurt, hungry, poisoned by man, dehydrated or dying. They cannot lobby their congressman if their habitat for centuries is being eliminated for American Dream purposes, and they cannot remind us about our stewardship responsibilities to look after them. These creatures are largely silent, unseen and subject to every whim a man may take to eliminate them.

By American Dream definitions, the wildlife is a very unsuccessful group, living poverty stricken, uneducated, unemployed, politically voiceless—but not to God, who created them, loves them and who has commanded us to look after them.

In *The Outermost House*, Henry Beston wrote in the 1920s about his study of the seashore and animal life during his one year residency in a small house on the Cape Cod beach. About animals he wrote:

> We need another and a wiser and perhaps a more mystical concept of animals. Remote from universal nature and living by complicated artifice, man in civilization surveys the creature through the glass of his knowledge and sees thereby a feather magnified and the whole image in distortion. We patronize them for their incompleteness, for their tragic fate of having taken form so far below ourselves. And therein we err, and greatly err. For the animal shall not be measured by man. In a world older and more complete than ours they move finished and complete, fitted with extensions of the senses we have lost or never attained, living by voices we shall never hear. They are not brethren, they are not underlings; they are other nations, caught with ourselves in the net of life and time, fellow prisoners of the splendor and travail of the earth. [Henry Beston, *The Outermost House, A Year of Life on the Great Beach of Cape Cod*, 24–25, Henry Holt and Company, First Owl Books Edition, 1992]

You throw a stone into a pond and its force sends out ripples affecting other areas of the pond. The effect of human avarice is now starting to ripple into distant places of our planet, destroying species, taking winter out of winter, producing drought, breaking up icebergs, shifting migration patterns of animals, causing many to leave our planet for good. Once extinct, they cannot come back.

As Christians, we are not "of this world," so we are responsible for living our lives in a manner that reflects the glory and the love of God, in whose Kingdom our names are now recorded. We are not human beings going through a temporary spiritual experience. We are spiritual beings going through a temporary human experience. Part of that spiritual experience is to be alert to what is taking place down here, mindful that we are not here alone, that we share an existence with other wonderful creatures who want to live healthy and nourishing lives just like we do.

Sadly these creatures are finding their lives caught up in the web of the American Dream, a nightmare that is extinguishing their habitat, taking away their food chain and destroying their lives, so that the American Dream can prosper and the ambitious can "get ahead." God has placed us with them for a reason, and our responsibility in these dangerous times is to look after those other creatures who cannot look after themselves. It is not just man who cries out, longing for God. Rather:

> The *creation* waits in eager expectation for the sons of God to be revealed. For the creation was subjected to frustration, not by its own choice, but by the will of the one who subjected it, in hope that the creation itself will be liberated from its bondage to decay and brought into the glorious freedom of the children of God. We know that *the whole creation* has been groaning as in the pains of childbirth right up to the present time. (Rom. 8:19–23)

> "This winter they are cutting down our woods more seriously than ever…
>
> Thank God, they cannot cut down the clouds."
>
> Henry David Thoreau, Journal, 1852

Conclusion

The American Dream is so firmly rooted in the American belief system as being good for life that it is very hard even to suggest the opposite. But the Dream is a consolidation of all of man's selfish needs, for: more money, more power, more things, more attention, suggesting that these must be obtained if life is to have significance, if "success" is to be achieved and if praise from others is to be garnered. This dogma has now worked its way into the heart of the American public, and into some churches, establishing standards for success and failure that are not established by God but by the fallen world.

The successful communication of the American Dream and the legions it attracts have been advanced by the nation's marketing industry. Its labels are compelling, painted in glowing colors to look beautiful, promising to supply all of a person's need through the purchase of things, wise investment decision making and setting other material minded goals that never mention God. But God will not permit the human heart to be lied to, so it still calls out to completeness, the need for fallen man to return to Him, no matter how much we have successfully gained from the world, no matter how successfully we have succeeded in living the American Dream.

Satan's tactics have not changed. They are the very same tactics he used to tempt man away from God in the Garden of Eden: "Take, eat," he says, "this apple I give you. It is of *my* world, and it will nourish you, give you wisdom. See its beauty! Here: this is *my body*, take, eat."

God provides another lesson about the fantasies of the American Dream and the culture it promotes: "Son of man, these men have set up their idols in their hearts, and put before them that which causes them to stumble into iniquity" (Ezek. 14:3, NKJV). As Christians we must be wise: we must not let the worldly outer steal away the spiritual inner. We must not get lost in the American Dream.